Part Three

Introduction

I have written *Language in Action – Spelling and Punctuation* to meet the practical needs of lower secondary pupils. The National Literacy Strategy will already have laid foundations in the primary classroom but secondary pupils need to consolidate and extend their spelling and punctuation skills in preparation for Key Stage 3 tests, and for GCSE and beyond.

The text is arranged in three sections (one each for Years 7, 8 and 9) with alternating full-colour information spreads and black-and-white photocopiable activity sheets. Each section is carefully graded to ensure natural progression and there are regular opportunities for recapitulation and revision. At the end is a list of high-frequency words that are commonly misspelt, which has been culled from years of teaching English in secondary schools and tertiary colleges and from marking GCSE examination papers. Pupils should be encouraged to learn these words by heart.

I have done my best to make the information sheets simple, direct and clear, and I am grateful to Harry Venning for his lively illustrations which reinforce my points so amusingly.

I have varied the form of the activities as much as I can both to sustain visual interest and to make the acquisition and reinforcement of punctuation and spelling skills a challenging and enjoyable experience. Some activities are focused exercises which test the topic being studied; others are consolidation exercises. Some are designed as pair activities; some would lend themselves to group discussion. From time to time, questions on spelling patterns and punctuation conventions have been set in the SATs manner and based on materials from a range of genres. All activities can be worked on an individual basis, and could usefully be set as homework assignments.

Angela Burt

Acknowledgements

With thanks to the following for permission to reproduce copyright material in this book:

© Times Newspapers Limited, 1997 for the extracts 'Buster loses his grip on TV fame' by Robin Young (24 October 1997), p.53 and '3lb 11oz apple is world's biggest' by Michael Hornsby (24 October 1997), p.81.

The Times Educational Supplement © Times Educational Supplements Limited, 1999, for 'The Chemistry of Daily Life' by Mary Cruickshank (1 January 1999), p.9 and 'Prop or Tool?' by Ian Thompson (12 March 1999), p.88.

Every effort has been made to contact copyright holders. The publishers apologise to anyone whose rights have been inadvertently overlooked, and will be happy to rectify any errors or omissions.

End stops

There are three end stops: the full stop, the question mark and the exclamation mark.

Use a full stop at the end of a statement.

Most people like chocolate.

Use a question mark at the end of a question.

How many teeth have you got?

Use an exclamation mark at the end of a shouted command or an exclamation.

Drop that gun!
Thank goodness you're safe!

You may think that using end stops sounds very straightforward but not everyone realises when a sentence *has* ended. Others are very careless and use commas instead of the appropriate end stops. Some people just rattle on and on, not using any sentence punctuation at all until they come to the end of a paragraph.

Test yourself. How would you punctuate this unpunctuated passage? Can you see that there are eight sentences in it?

come in sit yourself down by the fire let me take that wet coat where have you been all week I tried phoning you but you were never there have you been really busy tell me all the news will you have a cup of tea

Capital letters

Always begin a sentence with a capital letter.

The school will be closed for repairs.

Always use a capital letter for the pronoun 'I'.

I'm really sorry that I ate your chocolate orange.

All proper nouns begin with a capital letter.

Sarah spent New Year's Day in Dublin.

Use an initial capital in titles for the first word and all key words.

Have you ever seen 'A View from the Bridge'?

Each line of verse usually begins with a capital letter.

> Here lie I by the chancel door;
> They put me here because I was poor.
> The further in, the more you pay,
> But here I lie as snug as they.

From a Devon tombstone

Capital letters can be used for emphasis (sparingly!).

You should NEVER touch a light-switch with wet hands.

Capital letters are used in some acronyms.

PIN   personal identification number

CAT   computer assisted tomography scanner

NATO   North Atlantic Treaty Organisation

Be alert to the use of capitals in advertising and posters, on television, on packaging, as well as in books, newspapers and magazines.

Activities

1 Write out this passage using end stops and capital letters where necessary. (There are ten sentences.)

> jane knocked at the door was anybody there it was hard to tell she knocked again after a few minutes there was no reply suddenly a sash window was raised noisily above her head jane looked up an extremely angry man was glaring down at her what could she do she had to deliver the message

_____

_____

_____

_____

_____

_____

_____

_____

2 Circle the ten letters that should be written as capital letters in the passage below.

> We had arranged to meet at 11 o'clock in west street, outside woolworth's. I'd not seen teresa for years and years until we bumped into each other, purely by chance, at easter. We had been at school together and had been 'best friends'. I can see her now in the red and grey uniform of st brendan's. Then I moved from norfolk and we lost touch. I was amazed to hear that, like me, she was now working for british telecom. It would be wonderful catching up with all her news.

3 Acronyms are formed from the initial letters of the words they replace (e.g. laser: light amplification by stimulated emission of radiation). Some are written entirely in lower case letters (like laser); others are written entirely in capital letters or with an initial capital letter.

Write the acronyms formed from these words. Punctuate carefully. Use a dictionary if you wish.

a) surface to air missile _ _ _

b) absent without leave _ _ _ _

c) radio detection and ranging _ _ _ _ _

d) acquired immune deficiency syndrome _ _ _ _

e) random-access memory _ _ _

f) self-contained underwater breathing apparatus _ _ _ _ _

4

The extract below is taken from an article about a project that helps secondary students from all over the world compare notes about how chemistry affects their lives.

In pairs, read the passage and answer the questions that follow about the punctuation that has been deliberately omitted and the capital letters that have been underlined.

Natasha Felbrich, a 16-year-old-student from frankfurt, has no doubt about the importance of chemistry in our lives. '<u>W</u>e all eat bread,' she says simply. 'Bread is chemistry.'

She was among students from <u>G</u>ermany, the Netherlands, France, England and America at the Royal Society for Chemistry in London in november for the launch of '<u>C</u>hemistry in Our Lives', the first unit in the Science Across the World (S<u>A</u>W) programme

From 'The Chemistry of Daily Life' by Mary Cruickshank in
The Times Educational Supplement, 1 January 1999

a) Which word in the first paragraph should have a capital letter and doesn't have one?

_____

b) Which word in the second paragraph should have a capital letter and doesn't have one? _____

c) Where is a full stop missing? _____

d) Four capital letters have been underlined. Each has to be written as a capital letter for a different reason. Give the four reasons.

i) <u>W</u>e _____

ii) <u>G</u>ermany _____

iii) <u>C</u>hemistry _____

iv) S<u>A</u>W _____

5

Circle the correct spellings and write them in the spaces provided. Use your dictionary for reference if you need to.

a) suprise	supprise	surprise	_____
b) paied	payed	paid	_____
c) annoyed	annoied	anoyed	_____
d) mean't	ment	meant	_____
e) frightened	fritened	frightend	_____
f) compleatly	completly	completely	_____
g) reccomend	recommend	reccommend	_____
h) definatly	deffinitely	definitely	_____
i) suggest	surgest	sujest	_____
j) disappoint	dissappoint	disapoint	_____

Plurals (1)

The spelling of plurals in English can be a minefield, as you've probably already discovered.

It's really not worth trying to learn each plural form individually. Save a lot of time and effort by learning five basic spelling patterns that cover between them thousands and thousands of words.

Rule 1

Most nouns form their plural by adding -s:
doors, windows, superstitions, concerts.

Rule 2

Some nouns need an extra syllable (-es) to make them easier to say. You can always **hear** this extra syllable. It's needed after words ending in: -s, -x, -z, -sh, -ch, -tch:
buses, foxes, waltzes, dishes, churches, witches.

Rule 3

This rule covers **all** nouns ending in -y. However, you have to know the difference between vowels and consonants to be able to apply it.

Vowels: a, e, i, o, u
Consonants: all the other letters of the alphabet

Words ending in vowel + y, add -s in the plural:
day   days
guy   guys
monkey   monkeys

Words ending in consonant + y, change -y to -ies:
lady   ladies
baby   babies
opportunity opportunities

There are **no** exceptions to this rule.

Rule 4

This rule applies to nouns ending in -o. There are some exceptions, but not many.

Most nouns ending in -o form their plural by adding -s: commandos, pianos, zoos, discos.

A **few** nouns can be spelt -os or -oes in the plural (e.g. halos/haloes). You can't go wrong with these!

Some nouns *must* add -es in the plural. These exceptions will always be listed in a good dictionary but it's worth learning by heart any that you use a lot.

buffaloes	echoes
mosquitoes	cargoes
embargoes	potatoes
dingoes	heroes
tomatoes	dominoes
mangoes	volcanoes

Rule 5

Most words ending in -f and -fe add -s to form the plural: roofs, dwarfs, chiefs, handkerchiefs, cliffs, sheriffs, carafes, giraffes.

In **some** plurals, the -f changes to a -v- sound. You can always **hear** when this happens.

knife	knives
leaf	leaves
elf	elves
life	lives
loaf	loaves
self	selves
wife	wives
sheaf	sheaves
shelf	shelves
calf	calves
thief	thieves
wolf	wolves
half	halves

And four words can be either -fs or -ves:
hoofs/hooves, scarfs/scarves, turfs/turves, wharfs/wharves.
You can take your choice!

Activities

All the exercises on this page require you to write the plural form of each noun. (Look back at the rules on pages 10 and 11 if you wish.)

6 Test your understanding of Rules 1 and 2.

a) month _____   f) church _____

b) cupboard _____   g) consonant _____

c) box _____   h) crutch _____

d) stick _____   i) doughnut _____

e) letter _____   j) desk _____

7 Test your understanding of Rule 3.

a) city _____   f) donkey _____

b) alley _____   g) quality _____

c) ally _____   h) abbey _____

d) party _____   i) quantity _____

e) copy _____   j) eccentricity _____

8 Test your understanding of Rule 4.

a) kimono _____   f) echo _____

b) studio _____   g) banjo _____

c) potato _____   h) sombrero _____

d) contralto _____   i) photo _____

e) mosquito _____   j) hero _____

9 Test your understanding of Rule 5.

a) reef _____   f) cuff _____

b) loaf _____   g) roof _____

c) flagstaff _____   h) wife _____

d) shelf _____   i) chief _____

e) hoof _____   j) thief _____

10

a) tax _____   f) sandwich _____

b) knife _____   g) hero _____

c) kidney _____   h) day _____

d) radio _____   i) stitch _____

e) bailiff _____   j) soprano _____

11 Write out this recipe, adding end stops and capital letters where they are needed. Use the plural form of all the nouns in brackets. Set out your work clearly.

how to make lemonade

to make a pint of lemonade you need four lemons, four (tablespoon) of caster sugar and water 1) squeeze the lemons and pour the juice into a pint jug 2) add the sugar and enough boiling water to dissolve it fill the jug with cold water and put it in the refrigerator a delicious variation is to use half orange and half lemon fruit added to homemade lemonade improves the look and taste of it add any of the following: (strawberry), (raspberry), stoned and halved (cherry), a sliver of lemon peel, (slice) of orange or lemon, a thin slice of cucumber peel a few washed mint (leaf) can be added when you take the jug out of the refrigerator, where it must have been for at least an hour before you drink the lemonade

Adapted from *Something to Do* by Septima (Puffin 1966)

_____

_____

_____

_____

_____

_____

_____

_____

_____

_____

_____

_____

_____

_____

_____

_____

_____

_____

_____

_____

_____

_____

_____

_____

_____

_____

Commas (1)

Commas have special jobs to do within a sentence.

○ Commas are used to separate items in a list. (Whether you use a comma or not before the final 'and' is entirely up to you.)

Ben, William, Tom, Megan and Kayleigh are going to be on television.

We're going to need candles, matches, batteries for the radio, and paraffin if there's going to be a power cut for the whole weekend.

James packed his rucksack, made a few sandwiches, telephoned his uncle, left a brief note on the kitchen table and walked sadly out of the house.

○ Commas are used to separate terms of address from the main part of the sentence. (Sometimes you will need a pair of commas.)

My dears, I'm delighted to see you.

Answer the phone, Sally!

I regret to say, ladies and gentlemen, that our play tonight is cancelled.

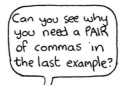

Can you see why you need a PAIR of commas in the last example?

Commas separate short asides and additions from the rest of the sentence.

Well, I will do what I can.

It's very cold today, isn't it?

His excuse, for what it's worth, is that he forgot.

Commas can be used to mark a short pause at a sensible point in a long sentence.

The play that we're seeing tonight is about a middle-aged man who has been fascinated by orchids all his life and who is now obsessed with growing the biggest orchid in the world, even though this has cost him his job and his family.

BUT REMEMBER . . .

● Never use a comma when you need a full stop.
  ✗ Mr Brown looked angry, he shouted at us.
  ✔ Mr Brown looked angry. He shouted at us.

● A comma must never separate a subject and its verb.
  ✗ The children, are going to be on television.
  ✔ The children are going to be on television.

Activities

12 In pairs, discuss which sentences below need commas. Use omission marks (∧) to show where you think they are needed.

a) Have you met my mother Mr Ponting?

b) You can plant cabbages sprouts cauliflower and broccoli in the next few weeks.

c) Which subject do you like best?

d) You look very pale Sally.

e) You should of course wash your hands before you handle food.

f) I'm afraid that I've forgotten your name.

g) Yes Katy is here.

h) Good morning everyone.

i) They've already got five dogs three cats a gerbil and a goldfish.

j) We'll do our best to arrange a Year 7 outing to 'Cats' this term but if all the matinée performances are fully booked and that's very likely we'll have to postpone our trip.

13 Read this short passage and answer the questions that follow.

'Just look at that rain! It's tipping down! Dozens of roads under water and it's going to get worse. If that's the case, and it obviously is, I really don't fancy driving all the way to Rochester this evening. What do you think, Emma? Should I plan to stay another night? Oh dear, I wonder what I should do for the best! I really do want to get back if I can.'

a) Explain why a pair of commas has been used in the fourth sentence.

_____

b) Why has a comma been used in the fifth sentence?

_____

c) Why has a comma been used in the next-to-last-sentence?

_____

d) Why is Rochester written with a capital letter?

_____

14 One sentence or two? Circle the five commas that should be replaced by end stops. Write out these sentences, correctly punctuated, in the spaces provided.

a) I'm sorry that I'm late, my mother forgot to wake me up.

b) Our new house should be finished by the end of August, much sooner than we expected.

c) I'll clean the blackboard, but you've got to empty the waste-paper basket.

d) Your cat is getting fat, are you overfeeding her?

e) Simon carried the lantern purposefully into the barn, he knew exactly what he was looking for.

f) Her room is always a mess, however hard she tries to be tidy.

g) We're going to have to economise, where shall we start?

h) Tinker is a wonderful guard dog, he terrifies everyone.

i) Three days after he bought the car, it was stolen.

_____

_____

_____

_____

_____

_____

_____

_____

_____

_____

_____

_____

_____

15 Test your spelling. These words need great care because they are often mispronounced and then spelt wrongly.

a) a _ _ _ _ c   (from north polar regions)

b) as _ _ _ _ t   (bitumen, or 'tar', used for road surfaces)

c) asp _ _ _ n   (popular remedy for the relief of pain)

d) ath _ _ _ _ cs   (sports such as running and jumping)

e) b _ _ _ _ _ r   (a thief who enters property unlawfully)

f) choc _ _ _ _ _ s   (the coating of these sweets is made from cacao seeds)

g) con _ _ _ _ _ _ _ _ _   (modern in style and design)

h) det _ _ _ _ _ _ _ e   (become worse)

i) disin _ _ _ _ _ _ e   (fall to bits)

j) event _ _ _ _ y   (in the end)

Homophones (1)

Homophones are words that sound the same but which are spelled differently (like *hear* and *here*). Computer spellchecks can't help at all.

Use these sentences as reference points and you'll choose the correct spelling every time.

| hear
here | You hear with your ear.
I am over here.
Here is the news. |

| its
it's | The dog wagged its tail.
It's too late now. (= it is)
It's been hot all day. (= it has) |

| knew
new | Kevin knew President Kennedy.
Do you like my new nightdress? |

| know
no | Kevin and Karen know Kevin Keegan.
No, I don't need a note.
I have no idea what to do. |

| their
there
they're | Their eyes are blue.
Wait for me over there. (here + there)
They're going to be late. (= they are) |

| to
too
two | Sam is learning to drive. (to drive = infinitive)
We're going to London. (to = preposition)
Can you come too? (= as well)
You work too hard. (= excessively)
Two and two make four. |

| who's
whose | Who's afraid of ghosts? (= who is)
Who's been eating my porridge? (= who has)
Whose socks are these?
He's someone whose jokes are never funny. |

| your
you're | Here's your supper.
You're always right! (= you are) |

Silent letters (1)

Words with silent letters can be especially difficult to learn by heart.
Use a variety of methods to help:

- Try mispronouncing the word by **saying** the silent letter to fix it in your memory

  e.g.   knit   **ker**-nit

- Think of other words in the same family where the silent letter is voiced.

  e.g.   crumb   crum**b**le

               bomb   bom**b**ard

- Use a different colour for the silent letter when you write it in your spelling notebook to make it more conspicuous.

  e.g.   sword

- Think of something silly that will remind you of the silent letter you need.

silent b	lamb	bomb	crumb	debt
	limb	comb	thumb	doubt

silent l	calf	walk	folk	would
	half	talk	yolk	should

silent k	knack	knee	knit	knuckle
	knock	kneel	knickers	knowledge

silent w	who	wrap	wrist	wriggle
	whom	wren	wrong	wrestle

Activities

16 Complete these words which each contain a silent letter.

a) n _ _b   unable to feel or move

b) _ w _ _ d   weapon with a long blade

c) t _ _ b   a grave, a stone coffin

d) w _ _ _ ch   to twist violently

e) s _ b _ _ _   delicate, not obvious

f) k _ _ _ d   to press and mould with the hands

g) s _ _ _ _ _ b   to give in or give up

h) d _ _ b   not able to speak

i) w _ _ _ _ _ e   small crease or furrow in the skin

j) w _ _ _ th   ring of flowers for a coffin or grave

k) _ _ _ b   a round handle or control button

l) c _ _ _ _   a tiny piece of bread

m) _ _ _ _ er   a reply or response

n) _ _ _ _ k   writing material made from soft white limestone

17 Fill the gap with the right word from the brackets.

a) We _____ exactly what would happen. (knew/new)

b) _____ in charge here? (who's/whose)

c) Are we allowed _____ use the photocopier? (to/too/two)

d) _____ very kind of you. (its/it's)

e) May I borrow _____ calculator? (your/you're)

f) _____ been more difficult than we expected. (its/it's)

g) Why do you always want to _____ where I'm going? (know/no)

h) I suppose _____ looking forward to the long summer holiday. (your/you're)

i) We could _____ in the distance the drone of motorway traffic. (hear/here)

j) _____ hoping to stay with us for a week. (their/there/they're)

18 Unscramble these words. Each contains a silent letter.

a) nmoals   sa _ _ _ _

b) kpshiecwr   sh _ _ _ _ _ _ _

c) bmperul   pl _ _ _ _ _

d) unclkke   _ _ _ _ _ le

e) fbtudolu   _ _ _ _ _ ful

19 In pairs, spot the silent letters. Circle all that you can find. There will be some that we haven't yet discussed!

John Brown had made up his mind. Talking had achieved nothing. He would write a letter to the *Daily Chronicle* on behalf of all old people like himself whose lives had been made wretched by this tax. He didn't write many letters these days now that his wrists and fingers and thumbs were half-crippled with rheumatism. Now where had he put his writing pad and envelopes?

20 Write out the passage below, correcting all punctuation and spelling errors. Compare your version with that of your partner.

The coachs will be leaving school tomorrow at 8 a.m. If your not hear by then you no that we'll have too go without you.

Bring a packed lunch, we shoud be able too eat our lunch by the river if the weather stays fine. Dress sensibly. There's quite a lot of walking if we're going too fit in holy trinity church *and* Shakespeare's birthplace.

We no you'll be on you're best behaviour during the performance no wispering giggling and unrapping sweet papers however, badly other school partyes behave!

It shoud be a good day, see you all tomorrow!

_____

_____

_____

_____

_____

_____

_____

_____

_____

_____

_____

_____

_____

_____

_____

_____

Apostrophes (1)

Apostrophes of omission

> Apostrophes (') are used to show where letters in contractions have been omitted.

I'm very sorry.   (I am)

Let's go.   (let us)

He's dyed his hair.   (he has)

You're very rude.   (you are)

It's my turn.   (it is)

Who'll help me?   (who will)

They didn't say anything.   (did not)

School finishes at four o'clock.   (of the clock)

Her sister's getting engaged.   (sister is)

My cat's had ten kittens.   (cat has)

Be very careful (with contractions involving *not*) to place the apostrophe where the letter is missing and not where the two words have been joined.

✔ didn't   ✘ did'nt

✔ don't   ✘ do'nt

✔ isn't   ✘ is'nt

Style

Contractions are used in everyday conversation and whenever you want to achieve a relaxed conversational style in your writing. If you feel a more impersonal formal style is appropriate, then avoid using contractions (just as you'll avoid using slang).

Talking point
Which contraction on this page is *never* written in full in modern English?

Possessive apostrophes

Apostrophes are used to show ownership.

the bicycle of William = William's bicycle

Here is a rule that will help you put the apostrophe in the right place *every time*.

- Find the owner.   ⟹ William
- Add the apostrophe.   ⟹ William'
- Add s if there isn't one.   ⟹ William's bicycle

It works with plurals too.

the rabbit of the twins = the twins' rabbit

- Find the owners.   ⟹ the twins
- Add the apostrophe.   ⟹ the twins'
- Add s if there isn't one. (There is!) ⟹ the twins' rabbit

the toys of the children = the children's toys

- Find the owners.   ⟹ the children
- Add the apostrophe.   ⟹ the children'
- Add s if there isn't one. (There isn't!) ⟹ the children's toys

Activities

21 Rewrite these sentences, using contractions.

a) She has not replied. _____

b) We would love to come. _____

c) He will regret this. _____

d) I have not read it. _____

e) Do not believe them. _____

22 a) Write out the paragraph below with the ten contractions correctly punctuated.

Didnt you know that well be leaving at the end of next week? I cant believe that nobodys told you. Im so sorry. Id have told you myself if Id realised. Its been a sudden decision but were sure itll be for the best.

_____

_____

_____

_____

_____

_____

_____

_____

b) Rewrite the paragraph, writing the contractions in full.

_____

_____

_____

_____

_____

_____

_____

_____

_____

23 Use your dictionary to find the longer words of which these are shortened forms.

a) bus _____

b) phone _____

c) pram _____

d) flu _____

24 Rewrite in a shortened form, using a possessive apostrophe.

a) the bag of my friend   my   _____ bag

b) the jobs of all women   all   _____ jobs

c) the screams of our peacocks   our   _____ screams

d) the petals of the rose   the   _____ petals

e) the cover of the book   the   _____ cover

f) the smile of your mother   your   _____ smile

g) the handles of the cups   the   _____ handles

h) the laughter of the men   the   _____ laughter

i) the wings of butterflies   the   _____ wings

j) the father of the princesses   the   _____ father

k) the barking of the dogs   the   _____ barking

l) the boyfriend of my sister   my   _____ boyfriend

m) the speeches of the politicians   the   _____ speeches

n) the loyalty of my friends   my   _____ loyalty

o) the success of his pupils   his   _____ success

25 Circle where apostrophes are needed in the sentences below and write the corrections in the space provided. Some sentences will not need any attention. Be on your guard!

a) My brothers girlfriend is very shy.   _____

b) All the childrens parents were delighted at the news.   _____

c) We've invited ten boys and eight girls.   _____

d) Have you met Mrs Brown, my sons teacher?   _____

e) It's my parents wedding anniversary tomorrow.   _____

f) There were enough cakes and sandwiches for all the pupils.   _____

g) We were delighted that Traceys grandmother won the prize.   _____

h) Both recipes need onions and peppers.   _____

i) My small brother thought he heard reindeers bells above the house on Christmas Eve.   _____

j) I thought that the bridesmaids dresses were nicer than the brides outfit.   _____

k) Sheilas mother promised to give us some apples.   _____

l) The secretary refused to give me the managers name.   _____

m) The congregations attention was constantly distracted by the screams of the babies.   _____

n) The childs handwriting was untidy but the letters were well formed.   _____

o) Few mothers would want to economise on childrens shoes.   _____

Adding endings (1)

Adding endings is usually quite straightforward – you add them and that's that. However, as the characters at the top of the page have found out, three groups of words need more care.

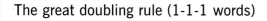
The great doubling rule (1-1-1 words)

This applies to words of **one** syllable, ending in **one** consonant with **one** vowel in front.

Double the final consonant when adding a vowel ending (an ending beginning with a vowel).	
spot + ed	spotted
sin + er	sinner
drop + ing	dropping
There is **no change** when adding a consonant ending.	
spot + less	spotless
sin + ful	sinful
drop + let	droplet

Treat qu as one letter, and so quit + ed = quitted

Never double w or x (it would look very odd!). So we have rowing and taxed.

Did you know?

The letter y is sometimes a vowel and sometimes a consonant. It depends on the sound of it. It's a **vowel** at the **end** of a syllable or word.

mud + y = muddy

It's a **consonant** at the **beginning** of a syllable: yolk, yellow, beyond.

Magic -e rule

This rule applies to all words ending in silent -e.

Drop -e when adding a vowel ending:	
use + ing	using
craze + y	crazy
Keep -e when adding a consonant ending:	
use + ful	useful
sincere + ly	sincerely

- Drop -e with these eight words:
  whilst, wisdom, truly, duly, ninth, argument, wholly, awful.

- Keep -e for soft c sound (noticeable) and for soft g sound (gorgeous).

- Keep -e to avoid confusion (dyeing is different from dying).

Adding endings to -y words

With this rule, it makes no difference whether you are adding vowel or consonant endings. It's the letter before the y that counts.

vowel + y	
enjoy	enjoy/able
pay	pay/ment
consonant + y	
beauty	beaut/i/ful
early	earl/i/er

- Eleven exceptions: laid, paid, said, daily, gaily, slain, boyhood, dryness, shyness, slyness, wryness.

- Keep -y when adding -ing (try + ing = trying).

Skiing is the only word in the language with two i's together.

Activities

26 Do these word sums. All the words are 1-1-1.

a) big + er _____

b) sit + ing _____

c) hop + ing _____

d) glad + ly _____

e) scar + ed _____

f) dim + ly _____

g) rob + ed _____

h) put + ing _____

i) wrap + er _____

j) sad + ness _____

27 Do these word sums. All the words are magic -e words.

a) scarce + ly _____

b) care + ful _____

c) separate + ion _____

d) excite + ment _____

e) wave + y _____

f) safe + ty _____

g) dine + ing _____

h) grime + y _____

i) hate + ful _____

j) achieve + ment _____

28 Now test your understanding of the 1-1-1 rule and the magic -e rule.

a) Sheila was kneeling on the floor, _____ up the hem of her daughter's skirt. (pin + ing)

b) The dog was _____ for his master. (pine + ing)

c) The twins were _____ up and down. (hop + ing)

d) We were all _____ you could come. (hope + ing)

e) My aunt found the little rascal _____ up a telegraph pole. (shin + ing)

f) The sun was _____ but it was very cold. (shine + ing)

g) Class 3 are _____ a visit to the zoo. (plan + ing)

h) _____ wood is not as easy as it looks. (plane + ing)

i) There's someone _____ at the window. (tap + ing)

j) He was _____ the pages of my book together with double-sided tape! (tape + ing)

29 Add these endings.

a) mystery + ous _____

b) lonely + ness _____

c) mercy + ful _____

d) healthy + er _____

e) apply + ing _____

f) easy + ly _____

g) penny + less _____

h) satisfy + ed _____

i) supply + er _____

j) lovely + ness _____

30

Spot the mistakes. Write out this paragraph, correcting all the spelling and punctuation errors you find.

Anna wondered what her mother would like for christmas. Chocolates flowers slippers calendars and diarys were all so dull she wanted something that was exciteing but not to expensive. Men were actualy easyer to buy presents for. Her father for instance always wanted handkerchieves socks or ties. Then she had a brilliant idea. Shed *make* her mothers Christmas present. She would make her a beautyful reath useing holly and ivy from the garden her mother woud realy like that

_____
_____
_____
_____
_____
_____
_____
_____
_____
_____
_____
_____
_____
_____
_____
_____
_____
_____
_____

31

Here are some words that are very often misspelt because they are mispronounced. Supply the missing letters.

a) env _ _ _ _ _ ent   (surroundings)

b) eq _ _ _ _ ent   (things that are needed or used for a particular purpose or task)

c) exp _ _ _ _ ion   (trip made for a special purpose)

d) extr _ _ _ _ _ _ ary   (unusual or remarkable)

e) gov _ _ _ _ _ nt   (control or organisation of a country and its people)

f) grad _ _ _ _ _ y   (slowly, by degrees)

g) han _ _ _ _ _ _ _ _ f (square of material used to wipe nose)

h) i _ _ _ _ mation   (knowledge communicated and received)

Punctuating direct speech

> Inverted commas (speech marks) are used to enclose the actual words of each speaker.

'We are very grateful,' my parents said.
My parents said, 'We are very grateful.'
'We are,' my parents said, 'very grateful.'

Can you see also how the punctuation of the sentence is affected when the position of the direct speech is altered?

We'll illustrate these changes more fully, using a statement, a question and a command each time as examples. This means that you should be able to use them as reference patterns if you are ever in doubt about how to punctuate direct speech in your own writing.

Speech first, narrative second

'Your hair is too long,' said the deputy head.
'Is there a rule about it?' asked Darren in amazement.
'Don't answer back!' snapped Mr Grimethorpe.

Narrative first, speech second

Darren said, 'I've always had long hair.'
Mr Grimethorpe growled, 'Are you being impertinent?'
The deputy head ordered, 'Get it cut at the weekend!'

Speech interrupted by narrative

'Mum, I don't like my hair long any more,' said Darren when he got home, 'and I want you to cut it really short.'
'Is this a joke,' asked his mother, 'or are you serious?'
'Just cut it, Mum,' begged Darren, 'and don't ask any more questions!'

Now read this continuation of the conversation and note the points that follow it.

'Did someone say something about your hairstyle at school?'
'No, Mum.'
'Are you sure?' persisted his mother, convinced that there was more to all this than Darren was admitting.
'Nobody said anything.'
'Really?'
'Please, Mum,' pleaded Darren, 'don't ask any more questions. I don't want to talk about it. Even if Mr Grimethorpe and Mrs Green hadn't told me off, I'd still have wanted short hair. Please, Mum!'

- Notice that a new line is taken every time there is a change of speaker, **even if** the 'new' speaker says only one word.

- Notice that the inverted commas show where a speech starts and finishes. You don't have inverted commas around every sentence of the speech!

- Notice that you don't have to name the speaker each time. It's obvious from the layout above when it's Darren speaking and when it's his mother.

Activities

32 In pairs, discuss the punctuation of these 'speech first, narrative second' sentences and then write them out carefully.

a) are you hungry my mother asked

b) the match has been cancelled the captain said

c) ill never save as much as that my small brother said sadly

d) stop fooling around shouted sarah

e) whats the time asked my grandfather suddenly

33 In pairs, discuss the punctuation of these 'narrative first, speech second' sentences and write them out carefully.

a) i asked her bluntly don't you believe me

b) they all shouted excitedly come over here

c) my father just said youll have to ask your mother

d) my little brother whispered what are you buying me for christmas

e) maryama said sadly we are moving back to nigeria

34 In pairs, discuss these 'speech interrupted by narrative' sentences and write them out carefully.

a) how much longer they moaned before we get to liverpool

b) get down from that roof immediately shouted my father and put the ladder away

c) next weekend said erin were going camping

d) i am sorry i said but i am not going to lend you any more money

e) do you know my sister exclaimed what mrs stevens expects us to do in the holidays

35 Write out these conversations correctly punctuated and spaced, taking care to take a new line for a change of speaker.

a) are you coming with us I cant why not you know why not

_____

_____

_____

_____

b) im sorry im late we got held up in a traffic jam have you been waiting long a few minutes said michael michael youre just saying that no im not yes you are persisted elaine

_____

_____

_____

_____

_____

_____

_____

c) and what will you have madam id like the chicken casserole with new potatoes and broccoli im afraid we have no more chicken casserole madam

_____

_____

_____

_____

_____

d) have you finished your bedroom yet asked mum not quite well get a move on I want it finished before your aunt and uncle get here yes mum

_____

_____

_____

_____

_____

e) im the only person in my class whos never been abroad on holiday i cant believe that said his mother its true colin said can we go somewhere exciting this summer it all depends on what you call exciting commented mrs hughes.

_____

_____

_____

_____

_____

Commas (2)

In Part One, we looked at four basic functions of commas.

Commas are used to separate items in lists.

I bought pens, pencils, crayons and sketch pads.

Commas are used with terms of address.

Maariya, you must believe him.

Commas are used with asides and interpolations.

Sam's progress, I am delighted to say, is excellent.

Commas are used to mark a pause.

Mrs O'Leary put down her book reluctantly when she heard the car draw up and she limped painfully into the hall to open the door to her visitors, although she really didn't feel in the least bit welcoming.

We come now to three more complex functions that commas can perform within the sentence.

Commas are sometimes needed with adverbial clauses.

No commas are needed in this sentence:

He was late for school because he overslept.

However, if you turn the sentence around, a pause is needed before the main point is made.

Because he overslept, he was late for school.

Commas are used to enclose words in apposition.

My daughter, Martina, wants to be a nurse.

My daughter and Martina are interchangeable terms. The second is said to be in apposition to the first and is always separated by commas.

Here are some more examples:

My son, Matthew, is a dentist.
Prince Charles, the heir to the throne, is a keen gardener.
The rumour, that they have been arrested, is not true.

Commas are used with participles, and phrases beginning with participles.

Laughing, the children ran into the sea.

They slept soundly, exhausted by their hard work.

Talking point

The first comma in the sentence below is wrongly placed. Where should it be put?

They slept soundly, and exhausted by their hard work, didn't wake up until lunchtime.

Activities

36 Circle the places where commas are needed in these sentences. Some sentences do not need commas.

a) Unless you hurry up it will be too late to apply.

b) We'll have supper when you've finished your homework.

c) As she walked towards the bus stop he passed her in his flashy new car.

d) Sean has promised to paint the house when he comes home in the summer.

e) Although I see your parents' point of view I think you've made the right decision.

37 Write out these sentences, placing commas around the words in apposition.

a) Mary Wesley the novelist lives in Devon.

_____

b) My boyfriend my best friend's brother is backpacking around Australia for five months.

_____

_____

c) Year 8's form captain Kathleen Miller is very efficient.

_____

d) Dr Carson the headmaster of King Street Junior is taking early retirement.

_____

_____

e) Are you Helen Comer my new neighbour?

_____

38 Circle the ten places where additional commas are needed in the conversation below. (This tests your understanding of all the functions of the comma discussed on pages 34 and 35.)

'Mary do come in! I've not seen you for ages. How are you?'

'Oh I'm feeling pretty low. Two of the children Claire and Laura have had mumps Tom's in trouble again and to cap it all Rodney's been made redundant. I can hardly believe it. If we win the lottery this week we'll emigrate. We really will.'

'But you'd miss everyone surely? You can't be serious!'

'I've never been more serious in all my life,' whispered Mary looking close to tears.

39 Place the commas accurately in these sentences (sixteen are essential).

a) Panting with the unfamiliar exertion I eventually reached the top of the hill.

_____

_____

b) Alan drove carefully through the gates and then coming to a gentle halt beside the steps heaved a sigh of relief.

_____

_____

c) The little girl doing her best not to cry seemed to be in a great deal of pain.

_____

_____

d) Deirdre bundled the washing into the machine and slamming the door shut pressed the start button.

_____

_____

e) Worried by the news parents phoned the school for more information.

_____

f) Abdul insisted however that there was nothing wrong.

_____

g) Overcome by emotion the whole class sobbed.

_____

h) Even Karen an experienced cyclist found the race a very demanding one.

_____

_____

i) I agree with you Francesca.

_____

j) Kieran Stephen and Darragh have volunteered to cut the grass clean both cars and tidy the garage.

_____

_____

40 **Spelling revision**

Write the plurals of these nouns.

a) donkey _____   k) wife _____

b) piano _____   l) opportunity _____

c) hutch _____   m) inch _____

d) flagstaff _____   n) quantity _____

e) theatre _____   o) radio _____

f) alligator _____   p) shelf _____

g) city _____   q) tax _____

h) potato _____   r) soprano _____

i) stitch _____   s) handkerchief _____

j) baby _____   t) echo _____

Silent letters (2)

In Part One, we looked at words with the silent letters b, l, k, w:

| silent b | lamb, comb, thumb, debt |

| silent l | half, walk, folk, would |

| silent k | knock, knee, knit, knuckle |

| silent w | who, wrap, wrong, wriggle |

We now consider silent g, gh, n, s, t.
Read these examples aloud, noting each silent letter carefully but taking care not to voice it.

| silent g | gnome, gnu, sign, foreign |

| silent gh | daughter, eight, light, bought |

| silent n | autumn, solemn, condemn, hymn |

| silent s | aisle, isle, island |

| silent t | castle, listen, moisten, bustle |

How to learn them by heart

- It helps to distort the pronunciation of some words when you are trying to learn them.
  e.g. gnu   **ger**-nu

- Think of other words in the same word family.
  Perhaps the silent letter is voiced in them.
  e.g. sign   si**g**nature

- Write out the spellings, using a different colour for the silent letter(s).
  e.g. dau**gh**ter

- Think of something silly that will stay in your memory.
  e.g. An island **is land**.

Spelling numbers

There are many occasions when you need
to be able to write numbers in words.

When you write a cheque, for instance, the
pounds have to be written in words as well
as in figures. In legal documents, dates and
sums of money are written in words so that
there is no possible misunderstanding.

In essays and non-technical written work, the general rule
is to write numbers up to 100 (one hundred) in words, and
to show numbers above this in figures.

e.g. By the time he was **eighty-four** years
old he had composed **122** major works.

Some numbers are
tricky to spell. Take
particular care with
these:

four (fourth)	eighteen (eighteenth)
fourteen (fourteenth)	eighth (eightieth)
forty (fortieth)	nine (ninth)
five (fifth)	nineteen (nineteenth)
fifteen (fifteenth)	ninety (ninetieth)
fifty (fiftieth)	twelve (twelfth)
eight (eighth)	

Notice also that the compound numbers between **twenty-one** and **ninety-nine** need
hyphens.

Activities

41 Complete the gaps.

a) nei__bourhood

b) __naw

c) mis__letoe

d) __riggle

e) ni__tmare

f) mor__gage

g) colum__

h) ai__le

i) lis__en

j) __restle

k) campai__n

l) plum__er

m) __nuckle

n) nau__ty

o) apos__le

p) __nowledge

q) epis__le

r) s__ord

s) bou__t

t) li__thouse

42 What am I? In pairs, complete these words. (The silent letter is given each time.)

a) g _ _ _   a small biting fly related to the mosquito

b) _ _ _ b _   uncertainty

c) _ _ _ _ gh   a sledge

d) _ _ _ _ _ g _   from a country not your own

e) g _ _ _ _   to grind the teeth together in fury

f) _ _ _ _ t _ _   a letter, especially in the New Testament

g) g _ _ _ _ _ _   knotty, twisted and rough

h) _ _ _ _ t _ _   to make slightly wet

i) g _ _   a South African antelope with a head like an ox

j) _ _ _ gh _ _ _   a round or ring-shaped cake, usually deep-fried and covered with sugar

43 Word families. For each of these words with silent letters, give another word in the same word family where the silent letter is voiced (use a dictionary).

e.g. sign   signature

a) autumn   _____

b) resign   _____

c) solemn   _____

d) moisten   _____

e) condemn   _____

f) castle   _____

g) column   _____

h) assign   _____

i) design   _____

j) epistle   _____

44 Write in words. Remember to use hyphens when they are needed.

a) 29 _____   f) 45th _____

b) 50th _____   g) 12th _____

c) 88 _____   h) 15th _____

d) 98th _____   i) 44 _____

e) 9th _____   j) 19th _____

45 **Revision.** There are thirty spelling and punctuation errors in the sentences below. Circle each error and then write the sentences in full correctly underneath.

a) Amy and I are hopeing to go to germany in september.

_____

_____

b) Hell be twenty one next week.

_____

c) Saddly, although the rescue services did there best fourty four lifes were lost.

_____

_____

d) The stunned guests filed silently into the dinning-room

_____

e) I think its amazeing that we have'nt met before!

_____

f) Their was the usual interest as you may imagine, when the cast list was pined to the notice-board.

_____

_____

g) We decided that we woudn't stay, as there were so few people we new.

_____

_____

h) Unfortunatly, his parents are much to strict with him.

_____

i) Everybody know's what Amandas reaction will be.

_____

j) 'Would anyone like to come to 'Twelth Night' on Tuesday. I have a spare ticket She said.

_____

_____

_____

Punctuating titles

Use inverted commas around a title or underline it, remembering to begin the first word and all key words with a capital letter.

Year 8 are reading 'To Kill a Mockingbird'.
Who wrote 'The Memoirs of an Infantry Officer'?
Have you seen <u>Phantom of the Opera</u>?

Use either single (' ') or double (" ") inverted commas, but be consistent. Some people use double inverted commas for direct speech and single inverted commas for titles:

"I'm going to be the third witch in 'Macbeth'!" she told her proud parents.

In print, on the other hand, you will generally find that double inverted commas are reserved for titles. Alternatively, titles may be italicised. Look out for examples of both conventions.

Punctuating quotations

Use single or double inverted commas around quotations, but, once again, be consistent.

Try to fit short quotations into the sentence you are writing:
Romeo calls Juliet's hand 'this holy shrine'.

Tom's friends "came to jeer, but remained to whitewash".

● Notice the position of the full stop. Using quotations is different from punctuating direct speech.

Set out longer quotations slightly differently, using a colon.

> The final sentence of *Animal Farm* confirms our worst fears: 'The creatures outside looked from pig to man, and from man to pig, and from pig to man again; but already it was impossible to say which was which'.

From *Animal Farm* by George Orwell (Longman 1964)

When quoting poetry, remember to keep the line boundaries intact.

> There is a haunting, twice-repeated question:
> 'Do you remember an Inn,
> Miranda?
> Do you remember an Inn?'.

From 'Tarantella' by Hilaire Belloc in *The Verse of Hilaire Belloc*
(Nonesuch Press 1954)

Sometimes an oblique (/) is used to indicate line-breaks.

> There is a haunting, twice-repeated question: 'Do you remember an Inn,/Miranda?/ Do you remember an Inn?'.

The ie/ei spelling rule

Learn the whole rule. There are very few exceptions.

ie		
friend	shriek	
chief	believe	**i** before **e**
niece	achieve	

ei		
ceiling	conceive	
conceit	perceive	Except after **c**
deceit	receive	

ei		
eight	neigh	
freight	reign	Or when sounded like **a**, as in neighbour and weigh
weight	reindeer	

Main exceptions: either, neither, counterfeit, forfeit, heifer, height, foreign, leisure, protein, seize, weird.

Activities

46

Rewrite these sentences, punctuating the titles correctly.

a) I always enjoy watching have I got news for you?.

_____

_____

b) He's seen an interesting advertisement in today's daily telegraph.

_____

_____

c) How much does the evening standard cost?

_____

_____

d) Henry VIII is reputed to have written the words of greensleeves and set them to music.

_____

_____

e) Panorama and casualty have been going for years now.

_____

_____

f) We've got tickets for arms and the man at the Northcott Theatre this Friday.

_____

_____

g) My parents could hear you singing my way from the end of the street.

_____

_____

h) I used to love reading dandy and beano.

_____

_____

i) Shall I get the sunday times or the observer?

_____

_____

j) A woman of no importance by Oscar Wilde has been chosen as their main production.

_____

_____

47 Punctuate these sentences. There is a quotation in each of them.

a) tolstoys exact words are every unhappy family is unhappy in its own way

_____

_____

b) as the poet once said all heiresses are beautiful

_____

c) this simple four line poem shows a real understanding of a small childs bewilderment and jealousy mum is having a baby im shocked im all at sea whats she want another one for whats the matter with me

_____

_____

_____

_____

_____

_____

_____

d) in a midsummer nights dream egeus claims that lysander hath bewitched his daughter hermia

_____

_____

e) remember bellocs advice in one of his poems and always keep a-hold of nurse for fear of finding something worse

_____

_____

_____

_____

48 ie or ei? Apply the rule safely in every case.

a) n _ _ ce

b) conc _ _ ted

c) y _ _ ld

d) br _ _ f

e) c _ _ ling

f) b _ _ ge

g) v _ _ l

h) _ _ ghteen

i) rec _ _ pt

j) handkerch _ _ f

k) d _ _ gn

l) dec _ _ ve

m) bel _ _ f

n) d _ _ sel

o) hyg _ _ ne

p) rel _ _ f

q) v _ _ n

r) gr _ _ ve

s) th _ _ f

t) p _ _ ce

Prefixes (1)

> Prefixes are syllables added at the beginning of words or word roots.

pre + fix = prefix
under + ground = underground
super + sonic = supersonic

Negative prefixes

You can make a lot of words negative by using the right prefix.

visible	invisible
tidy	untidy
appear	disappear
understand	misunderstand

- Take care when adding in- and un- to words beginning with **n**:
  in + **n**umerable = i**nn**umerable
  u**n** + **n**ecessary = u**nn**ecessary

- Take care when adding dis- and mis- to words beginning with **s**:
  di**s** + **s**atisfied = di**ss**atisfied
  mi**s** + **s**pell = mi**ss**pell
  You *don't* need to double the s otherwise!
  di**s** + appear = disappear
  mi**s** + behave = misbehave

- The prefix in- changes when it's added to words beginning with **n, l, m, p, r**.

noble	(in + noble)	i**g**noble
legal	(in + legal)	i**l**legal
mature	(in + mature)	i**m**mature
patient	(in + patient)	i**m**patient
responsible	(in + responsible)	i**r**responsible

It makes them easier to say...

Number prefixes

Recognising the prefix at the beginning of a word gives you a valuable clue to its meaning and also helps with the spelling.

Here are some prefixes that indicate numbers. They have all come into the language from Greek or Latin.

| uni-
mono- | unicorn (a mythical creature with **one** horn)
monocle (a **single** eye-glass) |

| bi- | bicycle (a cycle with **two** wheels) |

| tri- | tricycle (a cycle with **three** wheels) |

| quad- | quadruplets (**four** children born at one birth) |

| penta- | pentagon (a **five**-sided figure) |

| hexa- | hexagram (a **six**-pointed star) |

| oct- | octet (a group of **eight** musicians) |

| dec- | decade (a period of **ten** years) |

| cent- | century (a period of a **hundred** years) |

| mill- | millennium (a period of a **thousand** years) |

| hemi-
semi- | hemisphere (**half** the world above or below the equator)
semi-conscious (**half**-conscious) |

| multi-
poly- | multicoloured (with **many** colours)
polysyllabic (a word with **many** syllables) |

| omni- | omnivore (an animal that eats **all** sorts of food) |

Activities

49 Form the opposite of these nouns by adding a prefix.

a) gratitude _____
b) advantage _____
c) convenience _____
d) truth _____
e) mortality _____

f) comfort _____
g) maturity _____
h) security _____
i) probability _____
j) honesty _____

50 Form the opposite of these verbs by adding a prefix.

a) agree _____
b) please _____
c) behave _____
d) pronounce _____
e) pack _____

f) approve _____
g) infect _____
h) connect _____
i) wind _____
j) possible _____

51 Form the opposite of these adjectives by adding a prefix.

a) legible _____
b) regular _____
c) polite _____
d) even _____
e) similar _____

f) frequent _____
g) expensive _____
h) natural _____
i) credible _____
j) possible _____

52 Supply the missing letters. (Remember, your dictionary may be useful here.)

a) dis _ _ _ _ _   persuade someone not to do something
b) in _ _ _ _ _ _ _ _ _   unwilling or unable to believe
c) dis _ _ _ _ _ _ _ _ _   to break into small pieces
d) im _ _ _ _ _ _ _   fair to both sides
e) ir _ _ _ _ _ _ _ _   having nothing to do with the subject
f) im _ _ _ _ _ _   perfectly still
g) in _ _ _ _ _ _ _   not able to be heard
h) dis _ _ _ _ _ _ _ _   (of clothes or hair) untidy, unkempt
i) ir _ _ _ _ _ _ _ _ _   not able to be proved false
j) dis _ _ _ _ _ _   to take something to pieces
k) in _ _ _ _ _ _ _ _ _   more than can be counted
l) un _ _ _ _ _   rude and rough
m) mis _ _ _ _ _ _ _ _   unacceptable or wrong behaviour
n) un _ _ _ _ _ _ _ _   not expected or seen in advance
o) ig _ _ _ _ _ _   knowing little about a subject

53 All these words have their prefix in common. Give the meaning of each word, showing how **three** plays a part in the meaning of each.

a) trilogy _____

b) tripod _____

c) triceps _____

d) tricycle _____

e) triangle _____

54 These words have the same root but different prefixes. Give the meaning of each.

a) monogamy _____

b) bigamy _____

c) polygamy _____

55 Supply the missing prefixes.

a) _ _ _ _ tonous   lacking in variety

b) _ _ _ _ _ tude   a huge crowd

c) _ _ _ _ _ thlon   a sporting competition with five events

d) _ _ _ _ logue   a long speech by one person

e) _ _ _ _ scient   knowing everything

f) _ _ _ _ ruple   to multiply by four

g) _ _ _ te   to join together to make one

h) _ _ ennial   happening every two years

i) _ _ _ que   only one of its kind

j) _ _ _ _ rille   an old-fashioned dance for four couples

56 Proofread the paragraph below and circle each error that you find. Write the corrections in the spaces at the side.

It alway suprises me that some
people plan there summer
holliday in the depths off winter.
Thats not are way. We decide on
the spur of the momment and
ring the ferry companyes to see if
they have eny cancelations.
Theres usualy no probelem but
somtimes were dissapointed and
have to change are plans. We now
that we have to be flexable.

_____

_____

_____

_____

_____

_____

_____

_____

_____

_____

_____

Hyphens

A hyphen (-) is half the length of a dash (–).

Hyphens are used to indicate word breaks.

A word can be broken at a sensible point at the end of a line with a hyphen and continued on the next.

- Take care to break the word between syllables so that the reader can easily put it together again.

  e.g. earth-quake; ex-cellent/excel-lent

- When breaking a word into two, avoid distorting the pronunciation of the whole. For this reason, **legend**, for example, is best divided as le-gend and not leg-end!

- Never introduce a second hyphen into a word that is already hyphenated. Break the word at its existing hyphen:

  ✔ bus-conductor   ✘ bus-conduc-tor

- Avoid breaking any words of one syllable.

  ✘ a-nd   ✘ lea-rn   ✘ bre-athe

- Always place a hyphen at the end of the line where you are breaking a word. It's a signal to the reader that there is more to come. You don't need another hyphen at the beginning of the next line.

Note: It's always best to avoid breaking words if you possibly can. Try to anticipate how much space you're going to need and start a new line if in doubt.

Hyphens are used in compound words.

Compound nouns
Many nouns are in the process of changing from being written as two separate words to being hyphenated, or from being hyphenated to becoming written as just one word. This can be confusing, as the stages inevitably overlap.

Be guided by your favourite dictionary but enjoy comparing entries from time to time:

wash basin or wash-basin?

head-quarters or headquarters?

waste-paper basket, wastepaper-basket or wastepaper basket?

Compound adjectives
When two or more words are combined to make
an adjective, they are hyphenated.

We're a very close-knit community.
I've found twenty-nine slugs in one lettuce.
She gave me her superior I-know-something-
that-you-don't-know smile.

Notice the difference in meaning between a hard working family and
a hard-working family.

Hyphens are used with some prefixes and suffixes.

- They can separate adjoining identical letters in two syllables: ski-ing, co-operate, re-enter.

- They can help avoid ambiguity: recover and re-cover, reform and re-form, recreation and re-creation.

Hyphens can suggest a range of figures.

It happened during the 1914-18 war.
Read pages 18-56 for homework.

Activities

57 Circle the word break you feel to be most appropriate, bearing in mind the convenience of the reader.

a) (reappear) reap-pear, reapp-ear, re-appear

b) (weather) wea-ther, weat-her, weath-er

c) (telephone) tel-ephone, tele-phone, te-lephone

d) (abacus) ab-acus, aba-cus, abac-us

e) (creature) crea-ture, cre-ature, creat-ure

58 Add hyphens where necessary in these sentences and circle their addition clearly.

a) For her twenty first birthday, Sally is going to have a motorbike.

b) With one well aimed shot, he won the coconut.

c) The little used path was very overgrown.

d) I wish we had a mid afternoon break

e) It's a never to be repeated opportunity!

f) Which twentieth century writers do you like?

g) Don't risk walking on seaweed covered rocks.

h) Ian shrugged his shoulders in a couldn't care less kind of way.

i) They both come from a comfortable middle class background and don't know what it is to be hard up.

j) Who wants to come to the end of term party?

59 Circle the form used in your dictionary.

a) co pilot, co-pilot, copilot

b) public house, public-house, publichouse

c) co education, co-education, coeducation

d) eye witness, eye-witness, eyewitness

e) glow worm, glow-worm, glowworm

f) good will, good-will, goodwill

g) hand book, hand-book, handbook

h) arm chair, arm-chair, armchair

i) video recorder, video-recorder, videorecorder

j) head teacher, head-teacher, headteacher

Dictionary used: _____

Buster loses his grip on TV fame

By Robin Young

BUSTER the nut-cracking crab has blown his chance of television stardom. A planned appearance on a wildlife show was scrapped after he lost a pincer trying to escape from his tank.

The 8lb crustacean, denizen of the Sea Life Centre in Weston-super-Mare, was due to be filmed for *The Really Wild Show* crushing walnuts in his powerful claws.

But the BBC Wildlife Unit has had to recruit an understudy after Buster's accident. Staff at the Sea Life Centre say the pincer will take a year or two to grow back.

Neil Tredwin, a curator, said: 'Buster still has one good claw to feed himself, but television cannot make a star of a one-armed crab. We are very disappointed.'

© Times Newspapers Limited, 1997

From *The Times*, 24 October 1997

a) Explain why **nut-cracking** (para 1) and **one-armed** (para 4) are hyphenated.

_____

_____

b) Why is there a hyphen in **under-study** (para 3)?

_____

_____

c) Why do you think **Weston-super-Mare** is hyphenated?

_____

_____

d) The title of the show (*The Really Wild Show*) in which Buster was to have appeared is italicised. How else could it have been punctuated?

_____

_____

e) Why is there a pair of commas around **a curator** (para 4)?

_____

_____

f) Is the apostrophe correctly positioned in **Buster's accident** (para 3)? Explain.

_____

_____

Tricky pairs (1)

| accept except | I accept your apology. (= receive)
 Everyone came except Justin. |

| bought brought | My aunt has bought a yacht. (from **buy**)
 We brought our pets to school. (from **bring**) |

| clothes cloths | Sadly your clothes don't fit me any more.
 This drawer is for dusters and floor cloths. |

| desert dessert | They drove across the Sahara Desert.
 We're having ice-cream for dessert. |

| dairy diary | He's allergic to milk and all dairy products.
 Anne Frank kept a famous diary. |

| does dose | Gloria always does her best. (from **do**)
 You need a dose of cough mixture. |

| lightening lightning | They keep lightening the load.
 The golfer was struck by lightning |

| loose lose | My little brother has a loose tooth.
 There's no need to lose your temper. |

| of off | Ben is the leader of the gang. (sounds like 'ov')
 Jump off now! |

| quiet quite | They were as quiet as mice. (= silent)
 My mother was quite worried. (= rather) |

| were where | They were hoping it would rain. (= past tense of **are**)
 Where are you going?
 I know where she is.
 Here's the house where I was born. |

Tricky suffixes

| -ful | When full is used as a suffix, it is always spelt -ful.
care + full = careful, beauty + full = beautiful |

| -ly | Just add -ly to the base word. If the base word ends in l, you'll have double l.
part + ly = partly, real + ly = really |

| -cal | -cal for adjectives: nautical, practical |

| -cle | -cle for nouns: icicle, bicycle, vehicle |

| -able
-ible | These suffixes are notoriously tricky. Here are some guidelines for when you have no dictionary to hand. |

- -able is more common than -ible.

- Use -able with whole words: washable.

- Use -ible with incomplete words: credible.

- Use your knowledge of other words in the same family:
  adapt, adaptation, adaptable
  comprehend, comprehension, comprehensible.

| -ant/-ent
-ance/-ence | These suffixes also are very difficult. Check in a dictionary when in doubt. Here are some rough guidelines. |

- People are generally -ant: sergeant, attendant.

- Nouns from verbs are generally -ance: appearance, reliance, attendance.

- Use -ant/-ance after hard c and g: significant, significance, elegant, elegance.

- Use -ent/-ence after soft c and g: innocent, innocence, intelligent, intelligence.

- Use -ent/-ence after words ending in -i: audience, obedient, obedience.

Activities

61 Circle the correct word. Refer back to the exemplar sentences if you wish.

a) The lad with the fair hair is the leader (of/off) the gang.

b) You're (quiet/quite) right to complain.

c) (Were/Where) did you put the key?

d) This part of the farmhouse was once the (dairy/diary).

e) We've ordered fruit salad for (desert/dessert).

f) Everybody laughed (accept/except) me.

g) The children (were/where) soaked in the downpour.

h) The house seemed very (quiet/quite) when everyone had gone.

i) The oven handle is getting very (loose/lose).

j) Gran's vase just fell (of/off) the mantelpiece, Mum.

k) Marva looks wonderful in casual (clothes/cloths).

l) We (were/where) very sorry to hear the news.

m) Camels are well suited to life in the (desert/dessert).

n) Brian is beginning to (loose/lose) hope.

o) I know that Aisling (does/dose) her homework as soon as she gets in.

p) What have you (bought/brought) with your Christmas money?

q) Let's count the seconds between the (lightening/lightning) and the clap of thunder that follows.

r) Mary (bought/brought) everything she needed for the fortnight in one small bag.

s) Will you (accept/except) an alternative colour?

t) I'm going to write the date in my (dairy/diary).

u) She was really (quite/quiet) rude about it.

v) James is the best (of/off) the bunch.

w) My mother knows (were/where) he lives.

x) Have you noticed how she's gradually (lightening/lightning) her hair in easy stages?

y) You're very (quite/quiet).

z) Guess what Simon (bought/brought) in the Oxfam shop.

62 Complete these word sums with confidence.

a) waste + full _____

b) use + full _____

c) hope + full _____

d) grate + full _____

e) sorrow + full _____

f) spiteful + ly _____

g) rare + ly _____

h) practical + ly _____

i) careless + ly _____

j) sincere + ly _____

63 -cal or -cle?

a) Harry's approach is entirely logi_____.

b) The only obsta_____ is the cost.

c) Not all women priests wear cleri_____ collars.

d) We were all hysteri_____ with laughter at the end.

e) You're too criti_____.

f) Draw a cir_____ with a diameter of 8 cm.

g) He hadn't the physi_____ strength to open the tin.

h) Have you read the arti_____ in 'The Echo'?

i) There's not a parti_____ of dust there.

j) Her latest hobby is breeding tropi_____ fish.

64 Add -ant, -ent, -ance, or -ence.

a) differ_____ recipes

b) suffici_____ information

c) innoc_____ victims

d) ignor_____ behaviour

e) a radi_____ smile

f) neat appear_____

g) Garden of Remembr_____

h) frequ_____ interruptions

i) adolesc_____ readers

j) intellig_____ comments

k) a responsive audi_____

l) signific_____ looks

m) mysterious disappear_____

n) persist_____ efforts

o) refer_____ library

p) an import_____ point

q) sitting ten_____

r) arrog_____ behaviour

s) eloqu_____ speech

t) conveni_____ height

u) a lifetime's experi_____

v) leni_____ sentence

w) insur_____ policy

x) emin_____ statesman

y) pleas_____ smile

z) extravag_____ gift

65 -able or -ible?

a) We are not respons_____ for our children's debts.

b) Is the Severn a navig_____ river?

c) Her whisper was clearly aud_____.

d) The two friends were insepar_____.

e) The cabbage is a versatile veget_____.

f) Charles is a sens_____ child.

g) Your writing is almost illeg_____.

h) All the equipment is easily port_____.

i) It was an unforgett_____ occasion.

j) The doctor says an operation is not advis_____.

Abbreviations

We abbreviate words in four ways: we clip, we contract, we use initials, and we blend.

Clippings

pub (public house), sec (second), phone (telephone), ad/advert (advertisement), flu (influenza), fab (fabulous).

- No full stops are needed with clippings.

- Apostrophes with clippings ('phone) are no longer necessary.

- Remember that clippings are slang expressions. Don't use them on formal occasions.

Contractions

I'm , you're, let's, it's, we'll, they'd

- Contractions are very similar to clippings but they always keep the first and last letter of the original words.

- Take care to place the apostrophe carefully.

- Contracted titles (Dr, Mr, Mrs) don't have to have full stops. It's optional.

- The contraction, o'clock, is the accepted form.

Initialisms

VIP (Very Important Person), EU (European Union), VCR (Video Cassette Recorder), LA (Los Angeles).

- Consult your dictionary to check whether full stops are needed. The trend is not to use them in most cases.

Acronyms

AIDS or Aids (Acquired Immune Deficiency Syndrome), ASH (Action on Smoking and Health)

- When initialisms result in a pronounceable single word, they are called **acronyms**.

- Check in your dictionary to see where capital letters and lower case are required.

Blends

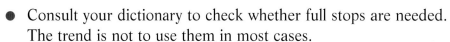

motel (motor + hotel), brunch (breakfast + lunch), smog (smoke + fog), camcorder (video camera and recorder)

- When blends are widely used, they become acceptable in formal writing and speech.

Homophones (2)

You will remember that homophones are words with the same sounds but with different spellings. Look carefully at these.

allowed aloud	Are we allowed to smoke? Dana screamed aloud.

boarder border	Matthew is a weekly boarder at the school. Why not plant a border of tulips? The car was searched at the Spanish border.

buy by	I'll buy the fruit tomorrow. (= purchase) The poem is written by Andrew Motion.

check cheque	Now check your work carefully. I'll write you a cheque for £100.

draw drawer	Draw a circle and then a square. Jim keeps his socks in the top drawer.

hole whole	You must have a hole in your pocket. Stuart has eaten the whole cake!

meter metre	I've already put £2 in the meter. A metre is approximately 39.4 inches.

passed past	Noreen has passed the driving test. (= succeeded in) They passed the photographs around the class. Paul has just passed the house. (= gone by) Your past will catch up with you one day. Have you any past papers? (= of earlier exams) Deirdre ran past without speaking. (= by)

seam seem	The shoulder seam is coming unstitched. They both seem very nice. (= appear)

weather whether	The weather forecast is awful. I don't know whether I can come. (= if)

Activities

66 Write these abbreviations is full.

a) fax _____
b) e.g. _____
c) P.T.O. _____
d) MP _____
e) c/o _____

f) rpm _____
g) demo _____
h) GP _____
i) ID _____
j) NHS _____

67 Which words are blended here? Use your dictionary to help you.

a) breathalyser _____ + _____
b) workaholic _____ + _____
c) heliport _____ + _____
d) bionic _____ + _____
e) Interpol _____ + _____

68 What are the derivations of these acronyms?

a) yuppie _____
b) radar _____
c) laser _____
d) scuba _____
e) sonar _____

69 Write these clippings in full.

a) specs _____
b) bra _____
c) fridge _____
d) mike _____
e) photo _____

f) disco _____
g) telly _____
h) bike _____
i) gent _____
j) exam _____

70 Write these 'school' abbreviations in full and then add some more. (Think of subjects, exam boards, clubs.)

a) lab _____
b) maths _____
c) gym _____
d) ICT _____
e) GCSE _____
f) _____ _____
g) _____ _____
h) _____ _____
i) _____ _____
j) _____ _____

71 Check your understanding of these homophones. Circle the correct word. Use the examples on page 59 as a reference guide.

a) We (passed/past) a wonderful sight on the way here.

b) Nobody will be (allowed/aloud) to leave the room during the examination.

c) The (draw/drawer) was locked and nobody could find the key.

d) I'd just finished weeding the flower (boarder/border) when it started to rain.

e) Unfortunately, there was a (hole/whole) in the petrol tank.

f) Could you fetch my camera from the dresser (draw/drawer)?

g) In the (passed/past) there would have been no cure.

h) There are no (boarder/border) restrictions as you leave Germany.

i) She tried darning the (hole/whole) but it looked dreadful.

j) I can never (draw/drawer) people.

k) Have we (passed/past) a newsagent's yet?

l) When did you last (check/cheque) the brakes?

m) I'm not (allowed/aloud) to go out during the week.

n) Do you sell material by the yard or by the (meter/metre)?

o) The (weather/whether) has been very disappointing.

p) Shall I write you a (check/cheque) or would you prefer cash?

q) You (seam/seem) very pleased with yourself.

r) My mother is planning to (buy/by) all her Christmas presents on the summer cruise.

s) Mrs Taber has invited the (hole/whole) family to stay for a fortnight.

t) Everyone on the estate is having a water (meter/metre) installed. They have no choice in the matter.

72 Test your spelling. These words need great care because they are often mispronounced and therefore spelt wrongly.

a) int _ _ _ _ _ ing   (holding attention, arousing curiosity)

b) lib _ _ _ y   (a collection of books, or place where they are kept)

c) mis _ _ _ _ _ ous   (playfully naughty)

d) pro _ _ _ ly   (likely to occur)

e) reco _ _ ise   (identify when see again)

f) sec _ _ _ ary   (office worker)

g) s _ _ prise   (unexpected or astonishing happening]

h) temp _ _ _ _ y   (lasting only for a limited time)

i) umb _ _ _ _ a   (portable device for protection from rain)

j) vet _ _ _ _ _ _ y   (to do with animal diseases and their treatment)

Letter layout

For both personal and business letters you can use either a fully blocked or a traditional layout, but keep to one or the other. Don't mix the two sets of conventions.

Personal letter: traditional layout

● Address sloped at 45°.

● Paragraphs indented to the same point (beneath the comma after the salutation or slightly to the left or right).

● Full punctuation above and below the body of the letter.

● Salutation and complimentary close appropriately matched:
Dear Mrs Giles ... Yours sincerely
My dear Anna ... With much love/Affectionately etc.
Hi, Steve! ... Cheers/Lots of love etc.

Rose Villa,

29 Green Close,

EXETER,

Devon.

EX2 4PF

Thursday, 18 May

Dear Mrs Giles,

    I am sorry that Tom has been absent from school for the last ten days.

    He's had tonsillitis and has really been under the weather. Fortunately, he's feeling much better now and the doctor says he can return to school today.

    Could he be excused games for the rest of this week?

        Yours sincerely,

        Anne Winton

◄ no name above address
◄ inverted commas optional
◄ comma after 29 optional
◄ block capitals optional
◄ full stop or comma
◄ no punctuation with postcode
◄ space
◄ date starts under first line of addre
◄ space

◄ capital letter for first word of complimentary close only

◄ no full stop

Business letter: fully blocked

● Writer's address aligned vertically.

● Recipient's name/title and address aligned vertically above salutation.

● No commas or full stops above and below body of letter.

● Paragraphs begin at left-hand margin.

● Complimentary close and signature on left.

● Salutation and complimentary close appropriately matched:
Dear Sir ... Yours faithfully (very formal)
Dear Sir ... Yours sincerely (formal)
Dear Mr Brown ... Yours sincerely (formal).

```
                                75 Tiverton Road
                                EXETER                    ◄ to save space
                                Devon EX2 4PF             ◄ space
                                                          ◄ formal date
                                18 May 2000               ◄ space


The Editor
'The Clarion'
Dockside
LONDON E1 9PY
                                                          ◄ space

Dear Sir or Madam
                                                          ◄ space

I read with dismay L.W. Adams' proposal
that all pupils of secondary age should
have four hours' homework every night.
                                                          ◄ space

My children have a wide range of out-of-
school interests and I consider these to
be essential to their social and cultural
development.
                                                          ◄ space

Surely we need a sensible balance?
                                                          ◄ space

Yours faithfully
Jack Watts
```

Activities

73 Mrs Winton could have written her letter (see page 62) using a fully blocked layout. On a separate sheet of paper, do this for her.

74 Mr Watts could have written his letter (see page 63) using a traditional layout. Write it out in this format, making all the necessary changes to positioning, paragraphing and punctuation.

75 Set out and punctuate this address, using *either* a fully blocked *or* a traditional layout. Assume that it is the writer's address, which will be written at the top of the letter.

> verity house 10 the avenue cosham portsmouth hants po5 9ew

_____

_____

_____

_____

_____

_____

76 a) Write this date as you would in a fully blocked business letter: 18/12/01.

_____

b) Which complimentary close would best suit the salutation: 'Dear Dr Harrison'?

_____

c) How much space should be left between the address and the date?

_____

d) Why is a postscript (P.S.) appropriate in a personal letter but not in a business letter?

_____

77 Address the envelope below to yourself, using *either* a traditional *or* a fully blocked layout. Make sure that you include your postcode.

78 Sharon has asked you to check her letter of application for the post of trainee technician. Unfortunately there are spelling and punctuation errors. Circle each error and write corrections in the spaces on the right.

> 2, Stakes Avenue,
> CHERTSEY
> Surrey,
> KT1 1SY
>
> 9th Febrary 2000
>
> The Human Resources Officer,
> Hayes and Berwick,
> 28-42 Halliwell road,
> LONDON, EC1 9SL
>
> Dear Sir or Madame,
>   I was very intrested to read your advertment for a trainee technitian in todays 'Chertsey Advertiser. This is just the sort of job that Ive been hopeing for.
>   As you will see from my c.v. which I enclose I have seven grade C GSCE passes encluding maths and one grade E in english. I have allways enjoied ict and science subjects.
>   At presant Im working parttime for my perants as a secertary in their sales office.
>   I do hope that you will let me come for an interveiw. I shoud realy like to work for hayes and berwick.
>   Yours Faithfuly,
>   Sharon Bell

_____
_____
_____
_____
_____
_____
_____
_____
_____
_____
_____
_____
_____
_____
_____
_____
_____
_____
_____
_____
_____

79 With your help, Sharon has impressed the Human Resources Officer, Mrs Ann Bond, at Hayes and Berwick. She invites Sharon to attend an interview on Wednesday 8 March at 10.30 am.
On a separate sheet of paper, and using a fully blocked format, write Mrs Bond's letter to Sharon.

80 Sharon is very excited when she receives this letter. On a separate sheet of paper, write the letter she sends to her grandmother, who lives abroad. Use _either_ a traditional _or_ a fully blocked layout, and make her letter sound relaxed and affectionate.

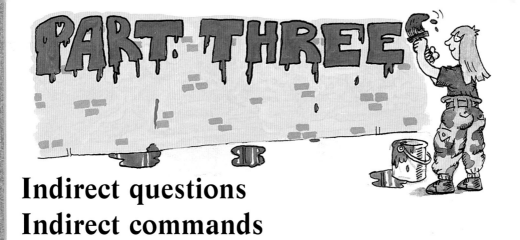

Indirect questions
Indirect commands

Direct question: 'Are you hungry?' she asked.
Indirect question: She asked me if I was hungry.

Direct command: 'Be quiet!' snapped the teacher.
Indirect command: The teacher ordered the pupils to be quiet.

> When direct questions and direct commands are changed into reported speech, they become statements. Question marks and exclamation marks are no longer needed.

He said that he loved her.

She told him not to be ridiculous.

He then asked her to marry him.

She refused and left.

● Be particularly careful with constructions beginning with **I wonder**.

I wonder if you are aware of the injustice involved.
I wonder if this is a mistake on your part.
I wonder if you can help me.

All three examples above are statements and require full stops and *not* question marks.

Apostrophes (2)

Possessive apostrophes of time

You will remember that apostrophes are used to show ownership.

Possessive apostrophes are also used in expressions of time.

an hour's delay   (**of** an hour)
ten years' hard work   (**of** ten years)
a moment's hesitation   (**for** a moment)
twenty minutes' exercise   (**for** twenty minutes)

More apostrophes of omission

Add to the list:

● Poetic contractions: o'er, e'en, where'er, 'tis, 'twas.

● Dialect: Wot's 'Arry bin doin'?

● Retail and marketing: salt 'n' vinegar, pick 'n' mix.

Talking points

You will see both: MP's and MPs
                    1970's and 1970s
                    'phone and phone.

The modern trend is to omit the apostrophe in these cases but conservative writers still love them. Look out for more examples.

Note that apostrophes are sometimes needed just to avoid confusion to the reader:
               Dot your i's and cross your t's.
               Mind your p's and q's.

Activities

81 Use an appropriate end stop.

a) Why are you smiling_

b) I love chocolate pudding_

c) Put your hands up and freeze_

d) When is your train due_

e) They asked me when I could start work_

f) I wonder if James will know the answer_

g) How are you feeling now_

h) I'm delighted that you're here_

i) Just leave me alone and go away_

j) Are you sure that you can trust him_

82 Change these sentences to reported speech.

a) 'Have we met before?' he asked Sandra.

_____

b) My grandmother smiled and said, 'May I join you?'

_____

c) 'Do stop arguing!' shouted her mother.

_____

d) 'Dad,' said Stephen, 'can you lend me £5?'

_____

e) 'Help!' cried the drowning man.

_____

83 Use apostrophes where they are needed.

a) five weeks holiday   _____

b) a days work   _____

c) six minutes delay   _____

d) eight years absence   _____

e) the centurys achievements   _____

f) twelve hours sleep   _____

g) a minutes pause   _____

h) three months salary   _____

i) six years supply   _____

j) the weeks Good Cause   _____

84 Write out these sentences, using apostrophes where they are needed.

a) This years expenses have been heavier than wed expected.

_____

_____

b) 'Come ere and wash yer ands. Its time to ave yer tea.'

_____

_____

c) Theyve agreed that a months notice will be sufficient.

_____

d) I wandered lonely as a cloud
That floats on high oer vales and hills.

_____

_____

e) Just think! In an hours time itll all be over!

_____

85 There are ten general punctuation mistakes in the passage below. Circle each error and write corrections in the spaces on the right.

It was nearly four oclock. Miss Wherly, headteacher of
Postgate High School was addressing the members of
her staff.

_____

_____

_____

Ladies and gentlemen I have some unpleasant news for
you but perhaps it wont be entirely unexpected. Pupil
numbers are falling and, regrettably, we have to lose a
member of staff.

_____

_____

_____

_____

The decision will have to be made in three weeks time.
I wonder if anyone here would consider early
retirement? Dont make a hasty decision now but there
could be advantage's for all of us if we could avoid a
compulsory redundancy. Its a sad situation.'

_____

_____

_____

_____

_____

Plurals (2)

We consider now those nouns that don't form their plurals according to any of the five rules we discussed in earlier pages.

Nouns that don't change in the plural

aircraft, cannon, bison, cod, deer, sheep, trout

Nouns with irregular plurals

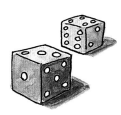

man – men
woman – women
child – children
ox – oxen
mouse – mice
louse – lice

die – dice
penny – pence
foot – feet
tooth – teeth
goose – geese

(but mongoose – mongooses!)

Compound nouns

The general rule is to make the most important word plural, whether it comes at the beginning of the word or at the end.

courts-martial
town clerks
mothers-in-law

man-hours
passers-by
bystanders

Sometimes two nouns are made plural:

women writers
menservants
Trades Unions

If there is no noun, simply add -s.

forget-me-nots
grown-ups
lay-bys

Talking point

Modern usage would favour armfuls, cupfuls, spoonfuls but you'll still see armsful, cupsful, spoonsful.

Foreign plurals

Some words that have come into the language from other languages have kept their foreign plurals; others have two plurals (sometimes with a distinction of meaning). Always check in a dictionary if you are uncertain.
Here are just a few examples.

Foreign words that have kept their foreign plurals

(Latin)	larva	–	larvae
(Latin)	radius	–	radii
(Latin)	bacterium	–	bacteria
(Greek)	crisis	–	crises
(Greek)	phenomenon	–	phenomena
(Italian)	graffito	–	graffiti
(Hebrew)	kibbutz	–	kibbutzim

Foreign words with foreign and English plurals

(Latin)	formula	–	formulae, formulas
(Latin)	syllabus	–	syllabi, syllabuses
(Latin)	curriculum	–	curricula, curriculums
(Latin)	appendix	–	appendices, appendixes
(Italian)	libretto	–	libretti, librettos
(French)	bureau	–	bureaux, bureaus
(Hebrew)	cherub	–	cherubim, cherubs

Mr, Mrs, Miss

These titles can be made plural. They are used in commerce and you may see them used in local newspaper reports of local events, but rarely elsewhere.
Mr becomes Messrs (from French *messieurs*)
Mrs becomes Mesdames (from French *mesdames*)
Miss becomes The Misses (e.g. The Misses Connor gave prizes.)
Miss becomes Misses (e.g. Misses Connor, Browne and Gray were present.)

Activities

86 Revise your understanding of regular plurals with this exercise.

a) Henry has lost two expensive _____ this month. (watch)

b) They have very happy _____ of their stay in England. (memory)

c) It's quite difficult to find a good selection of _____ in department stores today. (handkerchief)

d) Are politicians still being photographed with _____ at election time? (baby)

e) I love _____ too much ever to diet seriously. (potato)

f) Husbands and _____ are invited to attend. (wife)

g) I shall collect the _____ tonight. (photograph)

h) _____ got the hens again last night. (fox)

i) There are several refurbished _____ to let in the warehouses by the river. (studio)

j) They're a couple of loutish _____ , both of them. (oaf)

k) I think it's cruel to keep _____ as pets. (monkey)

l) How many _____ will it take to finish? (day)

m) The small children can sit on _____ . (bench)

n) Have you heard that no more free bus _____ are going to be issued? (pass)

o) Trevor's not very happy. He was given ten _____ this Christmas. (diary)

87 Test on all plurals! Make these nouns plural.

a) woman _____

b) quality _____

c) piano _____

d) thief _____

e) crisis _____

f) porch _____

g) oratorio _____

h) tomato _____

i) hanger-on _____

j) criterion _____

k) brother-in-law _____

l) abbey _____

m) salmon _____

n) oasis _____

o) butterfly _____

p) alga _____

q) press-up _____

r) bacterium _____

s) mongoose _____

t) editor-in-chief _____

88 Give the singular form of these plurals.

a) graffiti _____

b) candelabra _____

c) matrices _____

d) seraphim _____

e) media _____

f) vertebrae _____

g) memoranda _____

h) theses _____

i) châteaux _____

j) nuclei _____

89 Give the plural of each of these words and say from which foreign language each has come. Your dictionary will help you.

a) gateau _____ _____

b) terminus _____ _____

c) automaton _____ _____

d) apex _____ _____

e) dilettante _____ _____

90 Which plural? There is a distinction in meaning between the words in each pair. Your dictionary will help you choose the right plural in context.

a) I blame the _____ for bringing about the fall of the Government. (mediums/media)

b) My aunt believes that the spirits of the dead can communicate with those left behind, through _____ . (mediums/media)

c) The two feelers on the head of a butterfly are called _____ . (antennas/antennae)

d) On every rooftop, the _____ of television aerials could be seen. (antennas/antennae)

e) You'll find some really useful _____ at the end of the book. (appendixes/appendices)

f) The surgeon told me that he had removed thirty _____ this week. (appendixes/appendices)

g) There are no easy _____ for a happy life. (formulas/formulae)

h) Nobody expects you to learn all the chemical _____ by heart. (formulae/formulas)

i) I put the little _____ to bed at six o'clock. (cherubs/cherubim)

j) In the angel hierarchy, _____ come second in importance. (cherubs/cherubim)

k) Good reference books have _____ and full bibliographies. (indexes/indices)

l) I've forgotten how to multiply _____ in equations. (indexes/indices)

Colons

> A colon (:) always suggests that something directly relevant to the first half of the sentence will follow in the second half.

A colon can precede an explanation, comment or example.

The young doctor was exhausted: he had worked for twenty-two hours without a break.

The young doctor had worked for twenty-two hours without a break: he was exhausted.

There is only one solution: tough new legislation.

A colon can precede a list.

I bought some essential groceries: milk, butter, bread, sugar, eggs, bacon and sausages.

● Note that there should always be a summing-up word (e.g. groceries) before the colon.

A colon is used in a playscript to introduce dialogue.

Mona (anxiously): Where have you been? I've been so worried!

David (avoiding her glance): I have been to the police.

Semicolons

Semicolons (;) replace either full stops when they are used to join sentences or commas when they are used to separate items in a list.

Semicolons can join sentences connected in meaning.

I decided to move house; I also decided to hand in my resignation.
She is a fire-eater; her sister is a lion-tamer.

- There are distinct advantages in joining two short (and possibly jerky) sentences in this way, but use semicolons sparingly. Too many can become tiresome.

- Remember that only independent sentences can be joined in this way. The semicolon is replacing a full stop.

- Remember that the two sentences must have a connection in meaning.

Semicolons can separate items in a list.

I checked over the contents of the garden shed: one very old, very cumbersome wheelbarrow with a wobbly wheel; dozens of plant pots, unsorted; one heavy garden fork, much too big for me to use; a pair of secateurs, rusty and blunt; and dozens of bottles of strange-looking fluids, presumably designed to kill greenfly, blackfly and other sinister insects.

Talking point

Why are semicolons more effective than commas in separating items in the example above?

Activities

91 Circle the comma that could be replaced by a colon in each of these sentences.

a) I've cleaned every spoon in the house this afternoon, teaspoons, dessert spoons, soup spoons and serving spoons.

b) In the move, Simon lost all his tools, screwdrivers, chisels, saws, a plane, an electric drill, and several hammers.

c) All citrus fruits are rich in vitamin C, lemons, limes, oranges, tangerines and grapefruit.

d) You can make attractive designs by arranging pulses on a sticky background, dried peas, haricot beans, and, of course, lentils.

e) James packed what he thought he would need, a warm sweater, jeans, socks, pants and pyjamas.

f) Luckily, my father found a trolley for me at the station and put all my luggage on it, my trunk, my suitcase, an overnight bag, two roll-bags and my briefcase.

g) I've packed your toilet gear, razor, soap, deodorant, shampoo, toothpaste, toothbrush, flannel, and a towel.

h) She checked the contents of her handbag, purse, keys, comb, handkerchief, pen, and diary. They were all there.

i) The little garden was choked with weeds, dandelions, thistles, nettles, docks, and plantain.

j) Maeve has spent £30 on new make-up, two lipsticks, blusher, mascara, cleanser, nail-varnish and lip-gloss.

92 Tick the sentences where a colon is used correctly.

a) He's an excellent student: he deserves to do well. ☐

b) Henry's grandparents were very rich: they both had red hair. ☐

c) Leave me alone for an hour: it's getting cold, isn't it? ☐

d) I do have one complaint about the hotel: the water was only lukewarm. ☐

e) We can't help worrying: she should be back by now. ☐

f) There's only one thing you can do: tell me the truth. ☐

g) Do you have a choice of main courses: and would you have a table for two for 8 pm this evening? ☐

h) She enjoyed gardening: he loved fishing. ☐

i) There are two suspects: John Hall and you. ☐

j) You can't blame yourself for everything that happens: I'll phone again tomorrow when I have more time. ☐

k) I should love supper as soon as possible tonight: I'm starving. ☐

l) I need four hours' peace and quiet: without interruptions and distractions. ☐

m) There seems little point in Dana's continuing in mainstream education: she needs individual help. ☐

n) When you feel you can't cope any longer: it's worth seeking professional help. ☐

93 It is possible to use five semicolons in the passage below. Circle the places where they could or should be substituted for existing commas.

We dreaded her return from holiday. Out would come the photographs: views of her with Harold, smiling radiantly outside some tourist landmark, snapshots of the hotel dining-room with its ranks of small tables, all laid with identical cutlery, and decorated with identical flowers in identical vases, dozens of group photographs of smiling strangers, looking rather unpleasant and pushy, and endless, endless views of sandy beaches and beach umbrellas and sunburnt bodies. Why were we so uncharitable? We knew it was wrong, we tried hard to be kinder, we failed every time.

94 Colon or semicolon?

a) It was exactly as I had expected ☐ I had failed every exam.

b) The workers returned to work ☐ the strike had achieved nothing.

c) She opened the letter ☐ it was from her husband ☐ she read it without emotion.

d) One thing motivated her and one thing only ☐ greed.

e) He came ☐ he saw ☐ he conquered.

f) All the most valuable jewellery had been taken ☐ an emerald necklace with matching earrings, a pearl choker, a diamond brooch and at least ten antique rings.

g) Ethel (in some distress) ☐ I was nowhere near the dressing room. You must believe me.

h) We all knew what the basic problem was ☐ the fees were too low.

i) I was disappointed ☐ however, I could try again.

j) There'll be a school uniform check tomorrow ☐ everything must be named clearly and no excuses will be accepted.

95 Tick the sentences where the semicolon has been used correctly.

a) The reason for his failure is obvious; he was unwell when he took the exam. ☐

b) Having no desire to offend anyone; I left. ☐

c) I dread being alone with him; I don't like his sister either. ☐

d) This room needs redecorating; I'll do it for you, if you like. ☐

e) With no intention of defrauding anyone; Jason burned his grandmother's will. ☐

f) The wind increased in strength; it was very dark. ☐

g) Douglas asked to borrow my bike; as a special favour. ☐

h) The adults held their breath; the children slept. ☐

i) You should see a doctor; without delay. ☐

j) I loved the book; I borrowed it from the library. ☐

Adding endings (2)

The 2-1-1 spelling rule

This rule applies to words of **two** syllables, ending in **one** consonant preceded by **one** vowel: e.g. gallop, occur, budget, forget.

There's no problem when adding endings that begin with a consonant (forget + ful = forgetful) but complications arise when adding vowel endings. Sometimes you double; sometimes you don't.
It all depends on how the word is pronounced.

If the stress falls on the first syllable, just add the vowel ending:
GALLop/ing   BUDGet/ed.

If the stress falls on the second syllable, double the final consonant:
ocCURR/ed   forGETT/ing.

It sounds complicated, but persevere! It's a really useful rule that saves your having to learn hundreds of words individually.

Exceptions:

- Words ending in w, x or y *never* double, whatever the stress: e.g. re**lax**ing.

- Kidnap, worship, outfit *always* double whatever the stress: e.g. KIDna**pp**ed; KIDna**pp**er.

- Words ending in -l are tricky. Check in a dictionary unless you can remember that they usually double before vowel endings *except* in front of -ity, -ise, -ize.

- Be aware that the stress shifts in these five words, and spell accordingly: confer, defer, prefer, refer, transfer.
  CONference but conFER**R**ed
  PREference but preFER**R**ed.

Silent letters (3)

We have already considered words with these silent letters:

silent b	debt
silent l	would
silent k	knuckle
silent w	wriggle
silent g	foreign
silent gh	daughter
silent n	hymn
silent s	island
silent t	moisten

We can now consider silent c, h, p, u.

Read the examples aloud, noting the silent letters carefully but being careful not to voice them.

silent c	scissors, science, muscle, isosceles
silent h	heir, honest, rhythm, catarrh
silent p	pneumonia, psalm, pterodactyl, receipt
silent u	guess, guarantee, building, biscuit

How to learn them by heart

● Try appealing to your auditory memory by distorting the pronunciation of some words when you are trying to learn them: e.g. skissors (but don't spell the word with a k!).

● Try appealing to your visual memory by writing down the word you are trying to learn and using a different colour for the silent letter: e.g. guarantee.

● Try to think of other words in the same word family where the silent letter is voiced: e.g. muscle muscular.

● Try thinking of something silly that will stay in your mind: e.g. Yippee! A pterodactyl.

Activities

96 Complete these 2-1-1 word sums.

Follow the rule. There are no exceptions.

a) rivet + ing   _____

b) admit + ance   _____

c) equip + ment   _____

d) forgot + en   _____

e) regret + ful   _____

f) differ + ence   _____

g) drunken + ness   _____

h) limit + ation   _____

i) partner + ship   _____

j) acquit + al   _____

97 Complete these 2-1-1 word sums.

Be alert for exceptions to the rule.

a) allot + ment   _____

b) transfer + ed   _____

c) begin + er   _____

d) equip + ed   _____

e) worship + ing   _____

f) appal + ing   _____

g) pocket + ful   _____

h) annul + ed   _____

i) omit + ed   _____

j) destroy + er   _____

98 Test your understanding of the other rules for adding endings. Look back to pages 26 and 27 if you wish.

a) use + ful   _____

b) pit + ed   _____

c) sin + er   _____

d) pay + ed   _____

e) permit + ing   _____

f) sincere + ly   _____

g) early + er   _____

h) beauty + ful   _____

i) assess + ment   _____

j) real + ly   _____

99 Supply the missing silent letters: c, h, p, u.

a) r _ eumatism (aches and pains in the joints)

b) g _ ide (to show the way)

c) pasc _ al (relating to Easter and the Passover)

d) acquies _ e (to assent)

e) _ sychiatry (the study and treatment of mental illness)

f) antirr _ inum (a plant also called snapdragon)

g) g _ ardian (someone who stands watch and protects)

h) s _ ythe (a long-handled tool with a blade for cutting grass)

i) c _ ord (three or more musical notes played together)

j) r _ ubarb (plant with thick red stalks, usually cooked with sugar)

k) g _ erkin (a small cucumber used in pickles)

l) _ soriasis (a skin disease)

m) g _ illotine (machine used for beheading people)

n) s _ intillate (to sparkle, to be dazzlingly impressive)

o) _ tarmigan (a species of grouse)

100 Silent letter revision. Supply: b, c, g, gh, h, l, k, n, p, s, t, u, w.

a) assi _ nment

b) _ nash

c) hei _ _ t

d) si _ n

e) colum _

f) ras _ berry

g) _ seudonym

h) dis _ iple

i) k _ aki

j) des _ endant

k) ai _ le

l) _ nack

m) _ restle

n) dou _ t

o) cou _ d

p) honeycom _

q) resi _ n

r) _ narled

s) fas _ inate

t) desi _ ner

101 **Revision exercise**

Read the passage about the world's biggest apple and answer the questions beneath it.

3lb 11oz apple is world's biggest

By Michael Hornsby

A FARMER in Kent has grown the world's biggest apple, with a girth of $21\frac{1}{4}$ in. and a weight of 3lb 11oz. The monster Howgate Wonder comfortably exceeds the dimensions of the current champion, grown in Oregon in the United States, in 1994. It weighed a mere 3lb 4oz.

The Howgate Wonder is a cross between a Blenheim Orange and a Newton Wonder and is grown mainly as an exhibition and garden variety.

© Times Newspapers Limited, 1997

From *The Times*, 24 October 1997

a) List three words with silent letters used in the article.

_____

b) Why is Kent (para 1) written with an initial capital letter?

_____

c) Write in full:

3lb 11oz _____

$21\frac{1}{4}$ in. _____

1994 _____

d) Why is the apostrophe used in **world's** (title and para 1)?

_____

e) Make *variety* (para 2) plural. _____

Commas (3)

We have so far considered these seven uses of the comma:

1 Commas can separate items in a list.

You need butter, eggs, sugar, flour and water.

2 Commas are used with terms of address.

Mum, where's my electric drill?

3 Commas are used with asides and interpolations.

My parents, as you must realise, are a little eccentric.

4 Commas mark a pause.

She had heard that there was a generous grant available from the Department of the Environment for re-thatching old barns and cottages, and she decided to find out more about the scheme.

5 Commas are used with preceding adverbial clauses.

If you're interested, just give your name to Deirdre.

6 Commas are used with appositional words and phrases.

The two bridesmaids, Megan and Kayleigh, were dressed in blue.

7 Commas are used with participles and participial phrases.

All the children, shouting as loudly as they could, rushed into the overgrown garden.

● And to this list we can add the use of commas in the punctuation of direct speech, and the use of commas in traditional letter layouts.

We now take our study of commas further by considering their effect on meaning.

> 8   Commas are used with non-defining adjectival clauses.

Non-defining:

> The boys, who had revised for the spelling test, got full marks.
> (Well done, everybody!)

Defining:

> The boys who had revised for the spelling test got full marks.
> (Disappointing! Those who bothered to revise did well, but
> what about the slackers?)

> 9   Commas should be used before the final item in lists where
>   there is risk of confusion to the reader.

Name the five shops in this example:

> We shopped at Staunton and Greaneys, Faheys, Supervalu, Dunnes and Hughes
> and Jones.

Is the fourth shop Dunnes or Dunnes and Hughes?

Is the fifth shop Jones or Hughes and Jones?

An additional comma would make all clear:

> We shopped at Staunton and Greaneys, Faheys, Supervalu, Dunnes and Hughes,
> and Jones.

It is **never** wrong to use a comma before the final *and* in a list, and **sometimes** it is
essential.

Look out for other examples.

Activities

In pairs, decide where commas are needed in the sentences below and circle the places. (Ten essential commas are needed altogether.)

a) Fiona glanced hastily at the menu chose the dish of the day and lit a cigarette.

b) I seem to have lost my key.

c) We finished at last completely exhausted.

d) It's cold isn't it?

e) 'There'll be a final rehearsal today' announced Mr Sandiford 'immediately after school.'

f) We managed to sell our house thank goodness before prices dropped.

g) This is Mrs Macmillen our new deputy head.

h) We're disappointed in you Simon.

i) Have you ever read 'My Family and other Animals'?

j) Although the test was far more difficult than we expected we all did quite well.

Tick the sentences that need a pair of commas.

a) The girls in Year 9 who were wearing make-up were sent to the Head. (There are 115 girls in Year 9 and 27 were wearing make-up.)

b) The boys in Year 9 who chose astronomy as an option are on 'Newsnight' tonight. (Every single boy chose astronomy as an option.)

c) The children who were all away from home for the first time looked very miserable.

d) Do you think that people who are convicted of cruelty to animals should be allowed to keep a pet?

e) Her parents who were very much against letting her go to drama college have given in at last.

f) The tins of corned beef which were infected have all been returned.

g) Alison's dog which is the most vicious animal I've ever known is going to obedience classes.

h) Edward's beloved car which he's had ever since he left college is a complete write-off.

i) My husband who is a golf fanatic will be there, you can be sure.

j) The cottage which had been really neglected for years was the one they decided to buy.

104

Read the article below and then answer the questions.

Comma Brings Battle Over £100,000 Home to a Full Stop

A COUPLE won a court battle to keep their £100,000 dream house in the Lake District yesterday because of a comma.

A judge said the vital piece of punctuation meant Tony and Audrey Perry could not be evicted from their retirement home above Bassenthwaite Lake.

The Lakeland planning board claimed that rules designed to stop an influx of wealthy outsiders meant the bungalow could only be used by a local farmer or woodman. Their lawyers pointed out a clause which restricted the house to 'persons in the locality in agricultural or forestry work'.

But Mr Perry, the 59-year-old chief executive of Allerdale Council in Cumbria, knew the importance of reading the small print. His counsel William Braithwaite pointed out a comma after the word 'locality'. This meant that the house could be used only by people in agricultural work, in forestry, OR 'in the locality', he said.

He told the judge: 'With no disrespect to your honour I will quote an example of the relevance of commas from *Alice in Wonderland*.

Smiling

'The prisoner, said the judge, is a fool. Or is it: The prisoner said the judge is a fool? Commas do matter.'

After an hour's legal debate, Judge Donald Forster agreed, adding: 'This was a prosecution which should never have seen the light of day.'

The restriction on the house was imposed when it was built in 1981. The Perrys bought it four years later and were ordered to quit last October. They refused and were summoned to Carlisle Crown Court for yesterday's trial.

After the case Mr Perry left smiling but declined to comment.

A planning board spokesman said: 'We will look very closely at the judge's decision and consider whether there are any steps to be taken.'

From an article by Gerard Evans in *Today*, 17 December 1987

a) True or false? A comma saved the Perrys from eviction. _____

b) According to the planning board, which two groups of people only were eligible to live in the bungalow?

_____

_____

c) Which additional group did the Perrys' barrister prove could be included?

_____

d) Convert these two sentences to indirect speech.
'The prisoner,' said the judge, 'is a fool.'

_____

The prisoner said, 'The judge is a fool.'

_____

e) Why is a pair of commas used in the first sentence of paragraph 4?

_____

Homophones (3)

You will remember that homophones are words that sound alike but which are spelled differently. Do you know all these?

canvas canvass	He embroiders with wool on canvas. Her supporters will canvass everyone on the estate.

complement compliment	This ship now has its full complement. (= crew) Some verbs take complements and not objects. Copying your hairstyle is really a compliment. May I compliment you on your speech?

councillor counsellor	There are forty councillors on the Town Council. Your school counsellor will be able to help.

currant current	Do you like currant buns? Beware dangerous currents under the pier. Her current passion is line dancing.

formally formerly	They will announce their engagement formally tonight. He was formerly a boxing champion.

licence license	Show me your driving licence. (noun) Is the pub licensed for singing and dancing? (verb)

practice practise	Regular practice is what you need now. (noun) Practise the piano for ten minutes a day. (verb)

principal principle	His principal motive was greed. (= chief) The Principal had resigned. (= chief lecturer) I opposed him on principle. (= moral grounds)

stationary stationery	The car was stationary at the traffic lights. (= not moving) Pretty stationery is always a welcome gift.

Note also:

Noun	Verb
advice	advise
device	devise
prophecy	prophesy

(You can hear the difference.)

Tricky pairs (2)

affect effect	Smoking will affect your health. The effect was immediate.

allusion illusion	His allusion to my weight was very hurtful. It's an optical illusion that the line is straight.

bath bathe	They have a bath every morning. They bath the baby every evening. Bathe in the sea whenever you can. Bathe that wound in clean water.

born borne	Matthew was born in 1985. His mother has borne twelve children.

deceased diseased	Pray for all deceased relations. (= dead) The diseased branches were removed.

eminent imminent	Karen's uncle is an eminent scientist. (= famous) A thunderstorm is imminent. Take shelter.

human humane	We are all human beings. A humane person wants to lessen pain.

illegible ineligible	Your writing is illegible. (= can't be read) Your age alone makes you ineligible. (= unsuitable)

personal personnel	It's a personal matter and I don't want to discuss it. Send your completed application form to the Personnel Officer.

precede proceed	Spring and summer precede autumn and winter. Proceed with your speech. We will not interrupt again.

wander wonder	He'll wander off if you don't keep an eye on him. I wonder if you can help me.

Activities

Read the article and then answer the questions.

PROP or TOOL?

No one appears to have noticed the irony of a situation in which a government, professing itself to be committed to the effective use of information and communication technologies, then proceeds to argue for a restriction on calculators.

There are two illogical arguments used for banning or seriously restricting calculators in primary schools: our international performance; and the relationship between mental calculation and calculator use. Unfortunately, England does appear to fare much worse at number in international surveys than do many other countries. However, it is also unfortunate that this situation is accounted for by the argument that, since we in this country use calculators and do badly, and our more successful rivals do not, then banning their use will help us do better.

It is important to note that in the recent Third International Mathematics and Science Survey (TIMSS), Singapore, with the highest teacher-reported frequency of calculator use, did better than every other country in the world.

The second argument seems to be based upon a vision of primary-school children working through pages of sums all day using their calculators to find the answers. No one believes that calculators should be used in this way: children would learn nothing and their mental calculation skills would no doubt deteriorate.

But, importantly, there is contrary evidence that calculators can be used effectively to develop mental calculation.

© Times Supplements Limited, 1998

From an article by Ian Thompson (on calculators' bad press) in *The Times Educational Supplement*, 12 March 1999

a) What word(s) with the same meaning could be substituted for *proceeds* in para 1?

_____

b) What is the abbreviation for *information and communication technologies* (para 1)?

_____

c) What is the function of the colon in para 2? _____

d) What is the function of the colon in para 4? _____

e) What punctuation mark could be substituted for the semicolon in para 2?

_____

f) What is the meaning of *fare* in para 2?

_____

Make up a sentence using *fare* in a different sense.

_____

_____

Give a homophone for *fare* and use it correctly in a sentence.

_____

_____

g) The plural of *technology* is *technologies* (para 1). Find another word in the article that has formed its plural in exactly the same way.

h) Add -ing to these words:

argue   _____

fare   _____

note   _____

i) Find two words in the article with different negative prefixes. _____

_____

j) Use an appropriate prefix to make these words negative:

effective   _____

successful   _____

believes   _____

106 Choose the correct word from the pair in brackets. Look back to pages 86 and 87 if you wish.

a) Do you need a television _____ for every set? (licence/license)

b) I think you should try to _____ what you preach. (practice/practise)

c) He paid you a wonderful _____ . (complement/compliment)

d) We're making a collection of _____ slang. (currant/current)

e) _____ Brown is the committee chairman. (councillor/counsellor)

f) My parents _____ what had happened. (wandered/wondered)

g) Those tablets can have an unpleasant side _____ . (affect/effect)

h) It's all right to use slang in a _____ letter. (personal/personnel)

i) One _____ novelist donated £1000. (eminent/imminent)

j) Careful planning should _____ the actual writing. (precede/proceed)

k) An experience like that can _____ you for a long time. (affect/effect)

l) The poor lady was very confused. She had been _____ the streets for some hours. (wandering/wondering)

m) Damian found the _____ was too strong for him to swim against. (currant/current)

n) Your writing is not exactly _____ but it's very hard to read. (illegible/ineligible)

o) When you looked closely, you could see that the whole plant had been _____ . (affected/effected)

p) The Prime Minister's _____ to the Spice Girls was received in silence. (allusion/illusion)

q) Stretch the _____ carefully before you start painting. (canvas/canvass)

r) The Christmas Day _____ in the Solent has been cancelled. (bath/bathe)

s) Unfortunately, he crashed into a _____ car. (stationary/stationery)

t) She's training to be a marriage _____ . (councillor/counsellor)

Prefixes (2)

Recognising a prefix at the beginning of a word can give you a valuable clue to its meaning and help you with its spelling.

ante-/ant-	(before)	antenatal	anticipate
anti-/ant-	(against)	anticlockwise	antagonist
auto-	(self)	autobiography	automatic
bene-	(well)	benefit	benevolent
chrono-/chron-	(time)	chronological	chronicle
circum-	(around)	circumference	circumstances
contra-	(against)	contradict	contraception
fore-	(in front)	foreground	forecast
inter-	(between)	international	interrupt
mal-	(badly)	malignant	malnutrition
manu-/man-	(hand)	manual	manicure
micro-	(small)	microscope	microchip
post-	(after)	postscript	postpone
pre-	(in front of)	prefix	preview
sub-	(under)	submarine	subway

Dashes and brackets

Dashes can indicate hesitation.

I wonder – would you – I mean –.

Dashes can prepare for a climax.

Edith washed up, dried the dishes, and – collapsed.

Dashes can enclose a parenthesis.

I asked my father – he's an expert on Celtic archaeology – to date the samples.

Dashes can replace a colon in informal writing.

Ben did a few jobs for me – he mended the gate, changed a fuse, cut the grass, and so on.

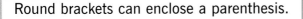

Round brackets can enclose a parenthesis.

I asked my father (he's an expert on Celtic archaeology) to date the samples.

Round brackets can separate information from the main structure of the sentence.

Charlotte Brontë (born 1816) was the eldest of the three sisters.

Square brackets indicate that something has been added to the original text by another writer.

'He [Willie] stumbled and droned and scribbled in his book like someone half asleep but Miss Thorne [the local librarian] knew that as soon as he had got rid of the book and had started working on the character of Scrooge he would be very different.'

From *Goodnight Mister Tom* by Michelle Magorian (Puffin 1983)

Activities

107 Give clear definitions of these words, underlining the part that relates to the prefix. Use your dictionary to help you.

a) chronic _____

b) prefabricated _____

c) autograph _____

d) posthumous _____

e) malicious _____

f) benefactor _____

g) intervene _____

h) antiseptic _____

i) posterity _____

j) microbe _____

108 Use your dictionary to help you find the meaning of these prefixes. Give an example of a word beginning with the prefix in each case.

a) hyper- _____ _____

b) hypo- _____ _____

c) trans- _____ _____

d) philo- _____ _____

e) mega- _____ _____

f) psycho- _____ _____

g) super- _____ _____

h) pseudo- _____ _____

i) arch- _____ _____

j) retro- _____ _____

109 Complete these words. Use a dictionary to help you.

a) circum _ _ _ _ _ ate   sail around (world)

b) contra _ _ _ d   smuggled goods

c) tele _ _ _ _ y   mind-reading

d) intro _ _ _ t   an inward-looking person

e) per _ _ _ ate   to make a hole through

f) inter _ _ _ e   to get involved in other people's business without being asked

g) ambi _ _ _ _ _ _ _ s   able to use both hands equally well

h) demo _ _ _ _ y   a system in which the people choose who will govern them

i) fore _ _ _ _ _ g   a feeling that something dreadful will soon happen

j) sub _ _ _ _ _ _ _ _ n   under the earth

110 Read the four extracts below and answer the questions that follow them.

'Are you sullen and obstinate?'

'No, ma'am, I am very sorry for you, and very sorry I can't play just now. If you complain of me I shall get into trouble with my sister, so I would do it if I could; but it's so new here, and so strange, and so fine – and melancholy –' I stopped, fearing I might say too much, or had already said it, and we took another look at each other.

From *Great Expectations* by Charles Dickens (Penguin 1965)

a) Why are dashes used here?

_____

And finally, I really must remind you
that moans are not allowed before midnight
especially near the staff-room. It's impolite
and disturbs the creatures – I mean teachers –
resting in despair and mournful gloom.
You there – stop wriggling in your coffin, I can't
bear to see a scruffy ghost –
put your face back where it was this instant
or you won't get to go howling at the moon.

From 'Assembly' by Dave Calder in *The Usborne Book of Creepy Poems* (Usborne Publishing Co. 1990)

b) Why does the speaker interrupt what he is saying in line 4?

_____

c) Why does he interrupt what he is saying a second time (lines 6 and 7)?

_____

When I was a little girl in Guyana we didn't have television (although Guyana has television now), so people had to find their own enjoyment. Our house was always full of friends who would visit us at night, sometimes just to tell stories. When they started to tell jumbie stories (ghost stories) there I'd be sitting hanging on to every word, feeling the goose pimples on my skin.

From 'No Television But a Lot of Friends' (abridged) by Grace Nichols in *There's a Poet Behind You* edited by Morag Styles and Helen Cook (A&C Black 1988)

d) Why is the first pair of brackets used?

_____

e) Why is *ghost stories* enclosed within brackets?

_____

Spellings worth learning by heart

These spellings are ordinary, everyday words that you are likely to use quite a lot. They are very frequently misspelt by GCSE candidates (and others!). It's really worth making an effort to learn them systematically, a few at a time. Once you've learned them, you'll know them for ever.

absence
accidental
accidentally
accommodation
achieved
across
addresses
advertisement
afraid
all right
also
among
amount
annoyed
anxious
apology
appalled
approached
argument
arrangement
athletics
attached

bachelor
beautiful
beginning
behaviour
believed
benefited
biased
Britain
broken
business

career
careful
carrying
century
certain
character

choice
collapsed
colleagues
college
colossal
coming
committee
comparative
completely
conscientious
conscious
convenient
criticism

decided
decision
definitely
description
desperate
detached
difficult
dilapidated
dining
disappearance
disappoint
disease

eighth
embarrass
enthusiasm
environment
equip
equipment
equipped
especially
eventually
exaggerate
excellent
excite
excitement

exciting
exercise
exhausted
expedition
experience
extraordinary
extremely

familiar
family
fascinate
favourite
February
finish
forecast
foreign
fortunately
forty
forward
frightening

gauge
government
gradual
gradually
grammar
grateful
guarantee
guardian

heard
honest
humorous
humour
hygiene

immediately
immensely
independence
indispensable
inflammable

information
in front
innocent
instal
installation
instalment
intelligent
intentions
interesting
interrupt
irrelevant
isosceles

jealous

knowledge

leisure
library
literature
lonely
luxury

maintenance
marriage
meant
medicine
Mediterranean
mentioned
metaphor
millennium
miniature
minutes
mischievous
moment
murmur

necessary
nephew
niece
ninety
noticeable
nuisance

occasionally
occurred
occurrence
officially
omit

omitted
opinion
opportunity
originally

paid
parallel
parent
parliament
pastime
perhaps
perseverance
pieces
pleasant
possess
possible
prejudice
privilege
probably
professional
pronunciation

quarter
questionnaire
queue
quiet

really
receive
recently
recognise (-ize)
recommend
refer
referee
reference
referred
regret
regrettable
regretted
repetition
restaurant
rhyme
rhythm
ridiculous

sacrifice
safety
sandwich

scarcely
secretary
seize
sentence
separate
sergeant
severely
similarly
simile
sincerely
something
souvenir
speech
successful
suggested
surely
surprise

technical
temporarily
tendency
tired
tomorrow
tragedy
tragic
truly
twelfth

unconscious
until
unusual
unusually
upon
useful
usual

valuable
vegetable
vehicle
view
vocabulary
volunteered

Wednesday
weird
woollen
writer
writing

First published in 1999 by:
Stanley Thornes (Publishers) Ltd
Ellenborough House
Wellington Street
CHELTENHAM GL50 1YW
England

99 00 01 02 03 / 10 9 8 7 6 5 4 3 2 1

A catalogue record for this book is available from the British Library.

ISBN 0-7487-4415-0

Layout and typeset by D&J Hunter
Illustrated by Harry Venning
Printed and bound in China by Dah Hua Printing Press Co. Ltd.